MW00618577

THE BEGINNING OF WEALTH

THE BEGINNING
OF WEALTH

Reach Financial Independence
Through the 7 Wealth-Building Behaviors

BRANDON K. MOORE

The Beginning of Wealth:
Reach Financial Independence Through the 7 Wealth Behaviors
Copyright © 2022 Brandon Moore
All rights reserved. No part of this publication may be reproduced or transmitted in any form or by any means, mechanical or electronic, including photocopying and recording, or by any information storage and retrieval system, without permission in writing from author (except by a reviewer, who may quote brief passages and/or show brief video clips in a review).

Disclaimer: The advice and strategies contained herein may not be suitable for your situation and should not replace the advice of a professional. If professional assistance is required, the services of a competent professional person should be sought. The author shall not be liable for damages arising here from.

This work depicts actual events in the life of the author as truthfully as recollection permits. While all persons within are actual individuals, names and identifying characteristics have been changed to respect their privacy.

ISBN (paperback):978-1-957812-03-8
ISBN (e-book): 978-1-957812-04-5

To my kids: Kate, Conner, Ian, and Sutton.
You are my legacy, my greatest contribution to the world!

CONTENTS

CHAPTER 1

INTRODUCTION TO THE 7 WEALTH BEHAVIORS

"The rich man's wealth is his strong city."
—Proverbs 18:11

On March 31, 1984, one of the first "reality TV" shows aired. *Lifestyles of the Rich and Famous,* hosted by Robin Leach, toured the homes and extravagant lifestyles of movie stars, professional athletes, business tycoons, and royalty. During its eleven seasons, I watched and dreamed about owning some of those celebrities' cars and homes. Of course, as a kid born into a lower-middle-class family in Irving, Texas, I thought my best hope for obtaining such wealth would be in becoming a professional athlete or actor. The only other option was winning the lottery—although at that time, Texas didn't even have a lottery.

Reflecting back on those alluring TV shows, I now know that many of the people featured could be described as either *old-money-rich* or *new-money-rich.* I also learned that the old-money-rich inherited their wealth from someone else, whereas the new-money-rich acquired their money within their lifetime. Neither are inherently good or bad.

Both can provide plenty, but there's a difference in their implications. The only way to stay old-money-rich, without the current generation building on what their parents left them, is to spend less than those assets earn. Some generational wealth seems to remain never-ending—despite heirs trying their best to spend every penny. Usually, however, the second or third generation succeeds in spending or losing it all.

Since most people aren't relying on old-money wealth to survive and thrive, this book isn't about that kind of wealth. Instead, we will explore new-money wealth—and the behaviors to attain it and pass it on to the next generation.

New Money

When Americans call someone "wealthy," they're typically referring to new-money rich, sometimes called *nouveau riche*. But unfortunately, the wealth we see from movie stars and lottery winners is a facade. Those celebrities who drive $400,000 cars and live in $15 million mansions are only as wealthy as their ability to earn—and often, their earnings don't stay enough ahead of their spending. Those who make $20 million on a movie and spend $20 million on lavish living, for example, have zero wealth.

Lottery winners are also great examples of new-money-rich. Seventy percent of lottery winners will declare bankruptcy within three to five years of winning their jackpots (Murray 2016). I've seen this firsthand, through a client who was a lottery winner. At around $3 million, his winnings were relatively small compared to the large jackpots that you see on the news. And when I met him, he had already lost half of that amount to lawyers, accountants, family spending, and taxes.

What the new-money-rich eventually learn is this: the person you were before the money is the same person as after the money. My client was an over-consumer before and continued to be an over-consumer after. If you don't follow the *seven wealth behaviors* before coming into a windfall, or getting a promotion, or whatever changes your status, you will struggle to change your behaviors after.

You don't need to depend upon inheriting your fortune and becoming old-money-rich. Nor do you need to hope to hit the lottery, or land a role in a blockbuster, or sign with the NFL to become new-money-rich. Becoming wealthy in your lifetime isn't about birthright or luck—and that's the change in mindset and behavior we will discuss in this book. It's accessible to anyone who is willing to do the work.

When my wife and I first married, we had twenty dollars between us. And we only had that because we had received our deposit back after turning in the U-Haul we had rented to move her belongings into my apartment.

At the time, we lived in government-assisted housing in Lockhart, Texas. I worked two jobs to make ends meet.

When I thought about getting married, I wanted to provide for both of us. I knew my future wife would probably have a job, but I didn't want us to rely on her income for living expenses.

My income goal was $1,000 per month. That's laughable now; even thinking of supporting two people on those wages seems ridiculous. To make matters worse, I had a car payment of $250 per month.

But guess what? Our status changed. In less than fifteen years from April 13, 1996 (our wedding date), we became millionaires. How? We changed our mindset and exercised the behaviors I will reveal in this book.

When you make the *seven wealth behaviors* a part of your life, instead of waiting for wealth to be handed to you, they will mold you into a wealth creator. Even if you have inherited money or landed a large contract, these behaviors will help you retain that wealth. Combine the seven wealth behaviors and the E-Hero's Journey, and you will see your wealth accelerate.

The E-Hero, as you may learn from my past books, is the business owner who chooses the exciting life of the entrepreneur. Like the hero's journey in all the stories of fiction we love, the entrepreneur's journey is filled with challenges. The E-Hero overcomes them and moves toward a better life. You can read about the E-Hero's journey in my previous book, *The E-Hero's Journey: Your Guide to the Entrepreneur's Quest.*

What You Will Learn

In this book, we will discuss what it means to be wealthy. We will describe how to calculate your net worth and break through the preconceived notions of *rich people* versus *high-income earners*. Fortunately for you, you won't have to win the lottery, become a professional athlete, or be discovered as Hollywood's next actor. No, you only need to work hard, have a growth mindset, and practice the *seven wealth behaviors*, which are:

1. Vision
2. Discipline
3. Learning
4. Wisdom
5. Thrift
6. Investing
7. Giving

Before every chapter, I will quote a verse from Proverbs. Why? Because all the wealth behaviors can be found in that short book in the Bible. This isn't a religious book. But I recommend young entrepreneurs read a list of several books, and I always include the book of Proverbs.

In addition to the chapter beginnings, I may sprinkle select verses from Bible, and specifically Proverbs, within the discussion on the *seven wealth behaviors*. Please be open-minded to the wisdom of the wealthiest man ever to live. King Solomon had personal issues, but he also had a lot to say to young people about living well and finding financial and spiritual peace.

The Beginning of Wealth

The road to wealth begins with applying the seven wealth behaviors....

First, to move towards a life of true wealth, you must apply the first wealth behavior: *vision*. Without vision, there is no purpose or reason for true wealth.

When my wife and I married, I didn't have a vision of what our lives would be, other than happy with kids. Our greater vision developed over time, as leaders and mentors contributed to our lives. We began to see all that was possible through their guidance and example.

You, too, can develop a vision for your potential. When you write down such a vision and work toward it—applying the seven wealth behaviors—it can become a reality.

The *seven wealth behaviors* aren't a secret. They aren't based on new knowledge, nor are they complex.

Simple, though, doesn't always mean easy. Work will be required. Therefore, the second behavior you will learn is *discipline*. A disciplined mind leads to disciplined thoughts, which lead to disciplined actions. Discipline is the foundation on which all the remaining behaviors depend. For my wife and I to go from twenty dollars to multiple millions in net worth took discipline. A lack of discipline, on the other hand, could also cause accumulated wealth to dissipate.

Besides gaining discipline, along the path towards true wealth, you must learn how wealth is created. This occurs through adopting a lifestyle of *learning*, which is the third wealth behavior. Through books, mentors, and possibly formal education, you will learn the practice of continuous self-improvement. Additionally, you will discover a humble and teachable lifestyle.

What then should you do with that education? *Wisdom* helps you apply knowledge, with discernment. As the fourth wealth behavior, wisdom takes you to the next level. It separates you from those who learn, yet never apply that knowledge. Wisdom as a wealth behavior doesn't require mysticism or clairvoyance; it develops from experience and knowledge.

You should become wiser as you get older, but not everyone will. It's when you use what you learn that you gain wisdom.

The fifth wealth behavior is *thrift*. It sounds simple, budgeting and saving is necessary to build wealth, but being thrifty comes when all the previous behaviors are working together. Thrift creates a strong defense financially. It plans for spending and saving. It involves budgeting, negotiation, sacrifice, and avoiding the sin of comparison—which we will discuss. Thrift also comprises communication and agreement in your household. If you don't yet have a spouse but intend to marry, keep thrift in mind before choosing your mate. My wife and I have been blessed to be on the same page in this area for most of our married life. We couldn't have accumulated our wealth without agreement.

We will explore *investing* as the sixth wealth behavior. Going beyond saving and spending wisely, we will define investments and how to manage risk. We won't discuss specific products, but we will discuss how some investments create cash flow while others promise a future payoff. The behavior of investing takes advantage of the time value of money. We also will discuss how to overcome barriers to investing like fear, ignorance, and lack of resources. My family acquired wealth by preparing for our future, instead of waiting for blessings to fall from heaven—and I want to help you do the same.

Finally, we will talk about *giving*, the last wealth behavior. Giving to others and your community sows into the future of those around you. Not all wealthy people give, but they should. This behavior primes the spiritual pump to ensure future opportunities.

We also will talk about the law of *sowing and reaping* (also known as *seedtime and harvest*). Just like investing, you should start early, so you have plenty of seeds in the ground for your future. Likewise, we will explore *doing good* versus *feeling good*. In other words, it's more important to see results than to feel good about yourself.

Who Am I?

I've been a tax and business advisor for more than twenty years. My firm, BKM pc Certified Public Accountants, an entirely virtual firm, has employees in several cities in—and a few cities outside of—Texas. We exist to help businesses and their owners earn more, while keeping more of what they earn.

I've been a real estate investor for longer than I've been a CPA. As of the writing of this book, I own more than eighty housing units, mostly single-family houses and a few duplexes.

In addition to those businesses, I'm also a financial advisor and Certified Wealth Strategist© with BKM Financial, LLC. My life's work helps people see their financial goals become a reality.

As you read this book, you should evaluate your life and decisions. Are you behaving in a way that builds wealth, or pushes you towards the masses living paycheck to paycheck? When put into practice, these behaviors will have a wealth-generating effect on your finances. No matter your income level, when you begin behaving like a wealth generator, you will increase your wealth.

As we move through the chapters, as I mentioned, I will quote the Bible often. Again, this isn't a religious book. But I cannot deny the wisdom contained in the Bible. I am a believer, but these behaviors don't require you to get "saved." (Although I hope that you do get saved, because I believe your eternity depends on it.)

I want you to be happy, wealthy, and living your best life. Following the behaviors in this book will get you there financially. But they won't happen in a vacuum. You must decide to exercise these behaviors in your life—consciously applying what you learn. I believe you can do it!

CHAPTER 2

WHAT IS WEALTH?

"Wealth gained by dishonesty will be diminished,
But he who gathers by labor will increase."
—Proverbs 13:11

The poverty level for a family of four in the United States for 2021 is $26,000.00. For the rest of the world, it is $8,030.00, or $5.50 a day per person. More than forty percent of the world lives below the poverty level. Eighty-five percent of the world lives on less than thirty dollars per day or $10,950.00 per year (ASPE 2021; Ferriera and Sánchez-Páramo 2017; Roser and Ortiz-Ospina 2013; Schoch and Lanker 2020).

Even considering the cost of living in the rest of the world compared to the United States, we as a country are very blessed. That means if you are reading this as a US citizen, comparatively, you are wealthy. You have more things, earn more, and have more control over your life than 85 percent of the world. It may not feel like it some months (or even each pay period); however, most of our issues and financial problems are truly "first-world problems." That is, we may be complaining about our cell phone bill and Netflix subscription cost going up, while others wonder if they will eat that day. I write this not to make you feel bad or to diminish your challenges, but just to give you some perspective.

With that in mind, let's define *wealth*. You can calculate your wealth as your assets minus your liabilities, also known as your *net worth*. If you and your spouse have a home with a mortgage, a 401k, a few cars with liens on them, calculating your net worth takes a few minutes. You list all your assets first. The cars should be listed at liquidation value or trade-in value. Your home value may be found on Zillow© or Realtor.com©. You should receive a statement from your 401k at least quarterly. (I recommend you calculate your net worth quarterly, but at the least annually.)

Let's explore an example. If you appraise your house at $350,000, you will add that to your 401k valued at $150,000 and your vehicles at $25,000 each. The total of your assets in that case equals $550,000. Then you subtract the mortgage of $280,000 and the liens on each car of $27,000, which brings your total liabilities to $334,000. Subsequently, your net worth would be $216,000. Congratulations, you have a positive net worth!

Unfortunately, many people don't pay 20 percent down on their personal residence. So, let's subtract $70,000 from your net worth. In addition, most young urban professionals have student loans. The average student loan debt for 2021 grew to just under $41,000 (Hanson 2022). If you have a master's degree, you probably have a little less than $71,000 in student debt each. Let's subtract $82,000 (for you and your spouse) from your net worth, for our discussion. Likewise, the average household owes $6,000 in credit card debt(El Issa 2022). Now, your net worth reduces to just $58,000. This is still a positive number, but you are not wealthy just yet. (We will define *wealth* shortly, by the way.) And with all of that debt, how much of your income would you be able to allocate to wealth-building activities?

Just like people confuse owning fast cars and fancy homes with wealth, per my opening examples, people also confuse high income with wealth. But they don't necessarily coexist.

Years ago, when I wanted to invest in an apartment complex, I went to a few of my clients and asked if they wanted to partner with me. After weeks of discussions and sharing the expensive appraisal fee, they both disclosed that they had no cash for the down payment. I was shocked. I knew their income, because I prepared their tax returns. One had an annual adjusted gross income (AGI) of two to three times my own. The other's annual AGI was five times my own. It was eye-opening. Even though their income levels were multiple times my own, my net worth and cash reserves were three times theirs.

Why was this the case? Because they spent every dollar they earned. They lived in homes valued two to three times ours and were members of the country club, with high annual dues. They drove new, high-end vehicles and went on lavish vacations.

And what were their investments? Little to none. I had perceived them as wealthy, just like many of you would. They had nice things, so I thought they *must* be wealthy. But I was wrong.

Dr. Thomas Stanley wrote, *The Millionaire Next Door: The Surprising Secrets of America's Wealthy* (with William D. Danko, PhD), and *The Millionaire Mind*. The first book describes what the average millionaire looks like in America, and the second illustrates the decision-making process of the wealthy. Dr. Stanley and his team studied thousands of millionaires in all areas of the country with various occupations and backgrounds. Dr. Stanley eliminates the stereotypes and preconceived ideas about the wealthy in America. Spoiler alert: their lifestyle doesn't mimic that of the "rich and famous"!

One thing that struck me in reading these books was the discussion of the abundance of first-generation millionaires (those whose net worth exceeds $1 million) and "deca-millionaires" (those whose net worth exceeds $10 million). This fact illustrates how you can truly become wealthy in this country. The United States of America is one of the few countries where it not only happens, but it happens with regularity. Don't let the class warfare news and entertainment media convince you that it is impossible to get ahead. It *is* possible. The chapters following will help you convert that possibility into a reality.

Closely tied to wealth is the concept of *success*. In my previous book, *The E-Hero's Journey,* I described my definition of success. Success is *enjoying what I do while having more than enough to meet my needs and the needs of others.*

To live a fulfilled life, you should strive for success, as I defined it. But when you pursue success and then add the *seven wealth behaviors,* wealth won't be far behind.

For this book, I want to define true wealth. *True wealth is having enough income-producing assets and avoiding liabilities to enjoy financial independence and freedom from the stress of day-to-day money issues.* I realize there's a lot to that statement, and it could be left up to interpretation—so let's unpack that, as we did our definition of *success* in my other books.

Financial Independence

What is *financial independence*, as it pertains to the wealth definition I just described? Financial independence doesn't mean that you have a million dollars in the bank or that you live off the interest and dividends of your securities portfolio. It means *you're not dependent on your job to sustain your lifestyle.*

Many small business owners become financially independent. The business, as an asset, produces revenue for them and their family. They may have some investments, real estate, or savings, but the business funds their lifestyle. The point when the business operates independently of the owner delineates between the *financially independent business owner* and the *dependent business owner.*

Sometimes, owning a small business means you own a job. It may be job security, but it hasn't broken through to financial independence. Building systems and processes, training a leadership team, and releasing your employees to carry the load takes time.

Enough Income-Producing Assets

Having enough income-producing assets means owning *passive income* assets like real estate, securities, and other investments that pay you while you sleep. Passive income derived from rents, interest, dividends, oil and gas royalties, book royalties, and the like sustains the investor without the investor's sweat and toil.

We will talk more about these investments in later chapters. For now, know that passive income is a crucial ingredient of true wealth for individuals who don't own a small business.

How much passive income do you need? First you should target an amount passive income to cover your living expenses. Your living expenses may keep financial independence out of your reach. For example, I know some friends and clients who always have the newest phone or drive a brand-new vehicle. How long do those things stay new? New lasts until the next new thing comes out. Unfortunately, these expensive habits and an undisciplined use of cash can keep true wealth forever on the horizon.

Offense. True wealth requires having a good offense and defense. *Offense*, in this case, refers to your ability to earn either passive or ordinary income. The genuinely wealthy acquire income-producing assets. Interest on certificates of deposit (CDs) is good, but residential rental income, when well-managed, is better—producing more to build your wealth.

My father-in-law, Larry, worked in the grocery business for more than thirty years. The store had been sold to different companies several times. Each time, Larry was given the option to roll over or cash out his retirement plan. Most of the time, he chose to cash it out—usually to help his kids or pay off credit cards. After those thirty years, he only had $6,000 in his retirement account.

When he quit the grocery business, we started a real estate partnership. Eventually, we divided up the properties. Larry took nine of them, which had been purchased using his equity in a duplex he'd purchased for his mother-in-law to live in one side while they lived in the other; I took nine, which we purchased without cash down. How did this turn out for Larry? He eventually earned more money from his rental properties, social security, and a small city pension than he ever did working at the grocery store. He was able to live well in his retirement.

Larry represents one example. Along the slope of risk lie several passive income choices. If we were drawing a graph, I would put your savings account and CDs on the left side, representing the least amount of risk. I would put securities like stocks, bonds, and exchange-traded funds towards the left of center. Then, as you move to the right and increase risk, you would find real estate investment trusts (REITs), limited partnership interests, and real estate. The riskiest investments would be your small business venture, at the end of the spectrum. (I don't see the small business as riskier than real estate, but most people do, which is why I'm placing them on the right-hand side of this graph.) Also, there might be alternative investments, options, and commodities somewhere between real estate and the small business venture, but I don't generally recommend those investments.

All of these produce some income. For financial independence, you should pursue the acquisition of *income-producing assets*, which is income that will replace your W-2 or self-employment income someday. We will talk more about these investments in chapter 8.

Defense. *Defense*, in the context of wealth-building, refers to budgeting and discipline in your spending habits. It's possible to be financially independent with a small amount of passive income, if you take steps to reduce your expenses. For example, many people these days buy tiny homes or recreational vehicles and live minimalist lifestyles.

Daniel Norris, a pitcher for the Toronto Blue Jays, lives out of his 1978 Volkswagen van, when he isn't on the road with the team. I have a friend from high school who converted a school bus (called a "schooly") into an RV and travels with her kids across the county. These minimalist lifestyles are the extreme. Honestly, I couldn't do something so bold, especially since I am slightly claustrophobic. But it can be done.

If you aren't the extreme minimalist, then you will need to work on your defense another way. Those who save and have a vision or goal improve their defense through budgeting and discipline. (You will notice some of the seven wealth behaviors being mixed into the discussion here! More of that is to come....)

Avoiding Liabilities

The truly wealthy avoid *liabilities*—also known as debt, in the financial sense. Consumer debt like credit cards and vehicle loans are liabilities that can create financial stress. Those "low payments" add up and can mean bankruptcy if you lose your job or revenues decrease.

Avoiding debt is extremely difficult in today's reality, however. If you need a vehicle, their high costs necessitate financing most of the time. It used to be that people haggled over the price of the car; now, they haggle over the payment.

Like most things, prices rise when the "cost of money" becomes cheap. This means when it's easy to get financing, the actual price paid for the purchase rises. The same happens with housing, college tuition, and business equipment. Our economy has been flooded with cash from low-interest rates or zero-interest rate financing and the government's monetary policy.

Unfortunately, people don't stop at financing their cars, homes, and education. They will finance their vacations or Christmas, if the credit card companies promise zero interest rates. In this case, these people aren't thinking about tomorrow, because of the allure of today.

Consumer debt promises your future earnings to a third party in order to enjoy the convenience of the day. The Bible says, "...the borrower is servant to the lender" (Proverbs 22:7). Don't get me wrong, not all debt is evil. It can be a tool. But like most tools, it can be used against you.

Avoiding liabilities means saving money to buy things whenever possible. It takes faith and patience to deny yourself the immediate gratification of having things now. We will talk about this mindset in the coming chapters.

Day-to-Day Stress of Money

Another verse in the Bible says, "Money answers all things" (Ecclesiastes 10:19). But does it? I think we could find multiple examples of people with money who still need answers. Instead, I think the author was saying that people often look to money to answer everything. While truly wealthy people enjoy their freedom from the day-to-day stress of money or the lack of money, they still have concerns about family, relationships, and more. Before you move into financial independence, you will find that many of your concerns regularly involve money issues. The seven wealth behaviors will help you eliminate at least any concerns that financial stress may bring.

Start taking a journal with you every day. In that journal, write down every time you worried about something. Then, after about a month, go back and classify those worries. You pick the categories, but money should be one of them. After this exercise, most people will confirm that they worried about money more often than anything else. Often, money concerns get interwoven into other concerns—such as about health, parenting, and more. For those married with kids, this is especially true. That should tell you to implement these wealth behaviors and see most of your stress fall away.

You don't need mounds of cash to live stress-free. But you must have a strategy so your mind and body will focus on the plan, instead of your wants.

It will take time for you to implement the *seven wealth behaviors* and see them change your life. In the beginning, my wife and I had plenty of stress. We managed our stress by relying on our faith in Jesus and staying diligent on defense, while building our passive income offense.

Let's revisit the definition of true wealth. *True wealth is having enough income-producing assets and avoiding liabilities to enjoy financial independence and freedom from the stress of day-to-day money issues.*

Is that something you want? Most of us would answer yes!

But when we ask, "What are you willing to do about it?" there's silence. Why is that?

It might be that your life hasn't yet reached a tipping point. You max out your credit cards, spend more than you make each month, have no savings or investments, and allocate income to some debt payments, but you still believe everything is fine. If that's you, this book can't help. But for those who don't want this lifestyle (and its stress) now or in the future—and you know that change is necessary—the *seven wealth behaviors* will help you.

Yes, you can choose to be wealthy by following the wealth behaviors in this book. I can hear people complaining already. "Not everyone can be wealthy!" or "People don't choose to be poor!" I don't want to sound harsh, but yes, they do. Some of you are getting angry at me right now. I don't blame you. When I was like most people, I would have gotten angry too.

There are many arguments posed today about why people are poor and why others are not. There's no doubt that some are born into wealthy families and should become wealthy. Yet, many offspring of the wealthy have ended up living paycheck to paycheck.

This book won't explore research about whether someone born into poverty can get out of poverty. I will simply say that everyone born in the United States of America is uniquely positioned with abundant opportunities. Yes, some schools are better than others and have more resources. But all the excuses posed don't consider the most critical factor: your ability to choose. For the context of wealth as we've defined it, no matter the obstacles and predispositions of your family, taking personal responsibility for your actions is the only factor that matters. Hundreds of people rise above their circumstances and attain wealth and success each year. If they can do it, so can you.

Have Faith

When I talk about true wealth, I'm not talking about net worth of over a million dollars or lots of nice things. Beyond the definition I've provided, I'm speaking about a belief, a mindset. Before you can be wealthy, you must believe that it can happen, and it can happen to you!

When I began writing this book, I considered *faith* one of the wealth behaviors. Then I realized it isn't a behavior. It is, however, necessary to move from where you are to where you want to be. You must believe that it can be done! The Bible describes faith as "the substance of things hoped for, the evidence of things not yet seen" (Hebrews 11:1).

Think about that for a second. It is a substance—not physically tangible, but real on a different level. The substance of faith changes your world. It is a knowing that cannot be explained with words. Faith expects you to accomplish what you set out to do, no matter the barriers or distractions. Fear says that if something can go wrong, it will, and it will go wrong for me.

Don't have blind faith or ignore facts and circumstances around you. Faith doesn't equate to denial. Rather, faith allows you to overcome those circumstances, because it doesn't give up. Wealth behaviors create results through the substance of faith.

When I was twelve to thirteen, life was rough. My parents divorced, and I had to wash my own clothes, cook for myself, and find my own way to school. My mother was wrecked emotionally and had checked out of life. A few times, our electricity went out because she "forgot" to pay the bill. I vowed to myself that I would never live poor again. That's when the drive was born. It wasn't until much later, however, that I found the substance of faith to get out of poverty. Even though I had decided I didn't want to be poor, I didn't know how to break the chains my circumstances had laid on me.

Later, as I read the Bible, I learned about the substance of faith. My mindset had to be trained to believe. Life tends to train people to doubt and fear. When you break free from those chains, you begin living!

Destiny Versus Fate

I believe that being wealthy is a choice you make based on faith in yourself, God, and your destiny.

Don't get confused between destiny and fate. Everyone has a unique destiny, while fate results from the choices you make. Your destiny could be to become a great writer or artist, but if you never write anything or pick up a pencil to draw something, you have chosen your fate. You have left your destiny up to that choice, unfulfilled.

Let's take a piece from pop culture to explain this point. In *Star Wars: A New Hope*, Luke Skywalker was the nephew of a small farmer on Tatooine. His destiny was to become the greatest Jedi in the history of the galaxy. When Ben Kenobi asked him to come with him on his epic journey, he could have said no. At first, he did say no, but circumstances and an inner belief that he was meant for something more compelled him forward. His fate could have been to die a farmer. Instead, he became the Jedi Master Kenobi knew he could be.

Some parts of your destiny depend on talents, such as if you want to become a singer, writer, or professional athlete. Yet being wealthy depends on something other than talent. It's a trait you can train yourself to become—through the essential *seven wealth behaviors*. Let this book help you train yourself to become a wealth-building Jedi! Okay, I'll stop with the *Star Wars* references...for now.

Give Up the Excuses

Excuses are what people without courage use to defend their choice to do nothing.

I've been training in martial arts on and off since I was fifteen years old. In that time, I've heard and given many excuses as to why I can't perform a move or am not as flexible as I should be. Personally, I struggle with physical limitations. I'm flat-footed, bow-legged, and have asthma. Despite my past excuses, those limitations only push me to train harder and find ways to overcome them. I won't let them be a crutch that keeps me from pursuing an art I love.

I admit that I've leaned on those excuses several times to explain to an instructor why I can't do something. Thankfully, I've had instructors who would not listen to my excuses and pushed me to try anyway. Once, during a fit test, I was fatigued and gasping for air. I wasn't having an asthma attack; I was out of shape. My instructor asked if I needed my inhaler or other medicine. I said no. He gave me a sixty-second break, and then I was back at it.

Building wealth is similar. You may have setbacks or limitations from past mistakes, but that doesn't mean it's time to quit. Take a second to gather your breath, and then get back at it. Don't look back. Look forward to what lies ahead.

The first wealth behavior is what all the other behaviors depend on. So, let's start this journey by talking about vision.

Chapter Summary: What Is Wealth?

- True wealth is having enough income-producing assets and avoiding liabilities to enjoy financial independence and freedom from the stress of day-to-day money issues.
- Financial independence means you are not dependent on your job to sustain your lifestyle.
- Having enough income-producing assets means owning passive income assets like real estate, securities, and other investments that pay you while you sleep.
- True wealth requires having a good offense and defense. Offense, in this case, refers to your ability to earn either passive or ordinary income. Defense refers to budgeting and discipline in your spending habits.
- Consumer debt like credit cards and vehicle loans can create financial stress. Those "low payments" add up and can mean bankruptcy if you lose your job or revenues decrease.
- Avoiding liabilities means saving money to buy things. It takes faith and patience to deny yourself the immediate gratification of having things now.
- You must have a financial vision and strategy so your mind and body will focus on the plan, instead of what you have or don't have.
- Before you can be wealthy, you must believe that it can happen, and it can happen to you!

- Everyone has a unique destiny, while fate results from the choices you make.
- Excuses are what people without courage use to defend their choice to do nothing. You may have setbacks or limitations from past mistakes, but that doesn't mean it's time to quit.

CHAPTER 3

THE FOCUS OF VISION

*"Where there is no revelation, the
people cast off restraint."*
—Proverbs 29:18

Somewhere between my senior year of high school and freshman year of college, I noticed that if I continued my current path, my life wouldn't have purpose. Two of my best friends also were drifting toward that same life. I loved them dearly, but I realized that I didn't want to end up as they would most assuredly become—without direction.

Ray and Devin were brothers. Devin was the oldest and had become friends with my older brother before befriending me. Ray was a little older than me. We had met as kids at church and spent hours together each weekend on spend-the-nights and kids' church events. Many Sunday afternoons were spent drinking strawberry milk and eating cookies at their house.

Their dad was the youth pastor at our church. By the time we reached middle school, they had moved away—first to

Broken

Arrow, Oklahoma, and then to Brownwood, Texas. A minister's life is like military life sometimes. After the Brownwood move, Devin and Ray's parents divorced—also like military life.

As the oldest, Devin finished school in Brownwood, then moved back to Irving. Ray followed. They lived with their grandmother on their mother's side, who we called "Ninnie-Ollie." (Their other grandmother was "Ninnie-B," just in case you wondered.)

The divorce took a toll on the boys. They had a sister, Jill, but she was so young, she was shielded from most of the chaos of the divorce. Yet the boys had seen everything and knew why the divorce was happening. That drove them away from the church and their parents, and toward a life of mere existence. As long as they had money for beer and weed, they didn't seem to need or want anything else.

Two years after graduating from high school, Devin still had no plan for his life. I didn't have much figured out at the time, but I knew that I wouldn't get anywhere if I didn't have a vision, goal, or plan.

What do you want? Have you put any thought into it? Some have, and some haven't. Those who haven't seem to just drift on the wings of chance. They are the ones you see all around you, without passion or purpose. The world has beaten them down, kicked them in the gut, and left them for dead. They are lost and don't know it.

Vision infuses life with purpose. When you see into the future and decide what it will look like for you, you begin to move in that direction. You make plans, you set goals, and you create your destiny.

Vision is the first, number one, wealth behavior. Act like you're heading somewhere! Behave with purpose! Rise above the chaos of life—those kicks in the gut or groin that will try to derail you.

With vision, you can keep moving forward. Without vision, you will do nothing, be nothing, and build nothing.

Dreams

Your vision starts with your dreams. Those dreams begin as a child, as you let your mind wander into what is possible.

As we discussed, this requires the power of faith. You must lay hold of that *substance of things hoped for* and the *evidence of things not yet seen.*

There is a caveat here. Your dreams must not only be possible, but possible for you. You can't dream of being a rock star, if you sing like a cat that's dying and can't play an instrument. If you aren't proficient in math, please don't dream of winning a Nobel prize in engineering and mathematics.

Dreams don't need to be fantastic to spark vision. You can dream of being the best in your chosen profession or having a two-story house with a white picket fence. The dream is just the beginning of the vision—working like a compass to help you find your direction. Dreams should provide the push that gets you moving forward.

Guess what? Dreams can change. They shouldn't change often, but they do change. Before I went back to college, my dream was to become a traveling evangelist. I thank God that didn't happen. I would have starved!

When I began the accounting program at Angelo State University, I dreamed of working as a chief financial officer

(CFO) for a church. At that time, all of my dreams were ministry focused. Each dream moved me forward—toward something in the future.

The dream starts the process that leads you to your vision. Your vision should include three intersecting circles: mission, values, and goals.

Your mission involves the direction and purpose of your life—your greater reason for doing what you do, closely tied to your ultimate outcome.

Next, your values define your absolutes, the lines you won't ever cross. Think of these as the lines that encompass you, outside of which you won't color!

Finally, your goals are the points along the way that will lead to your ultimate success. Without goals, your mission stays a dream. Your goals create markers that illuminate the path towards your ultimate mission.

Mission

What is your mission in life? In business? In your finances? In your family? Did you ever think about having a mission statement for each area?

For our CPA firm, our mission is *to help our clients earn more and keep more of what they earn.* It's a simple yet defining statement. It sets the boundaries for our decisions toward that purpose.

Personally, my mission involves *helping train and develop leaders within my family, friends, and clients to help them become the best version of themselves.*

What is your mission? How do you determine what that mission might be? In the context of building wealth for you and your family, you must decide on your *why*. Mark Twain said, "The two best days in a man's life are the day he was born and the day he discovers why!" No one can figure this out for you. It's something you must experiment with and discover yourself. You can use tools like the *Five Whys*, a *mind map*, or a life coach to help you, but the answer must come from you.

The *Five Whys* is a discovery tool that helps you get to the root of a question or issue. In context of finding your mission, start with stating what you do or want to do. Then ask, "Why?" Then ask again and again, until you find the root (Syzmczak et al. 2016). As an example, here's an excerpt from my previous book, *The E-Hero's Journey*:

> You might start with, "We make barbecue sandwiches, brisket, sausage, and sides." Then ask why? "Because we know how to make those better than anyone in town, and they sell better than hamburgers." Then ask why again? "Because our family gave us the recipe, we have perfected it, and we want our customers to share in the joy of good pulled pork and brisket." Why? "Because we are filled with joy when we see our customers smile after taking their first bite."
>
> After examining these responses, your purpose statement might be: "To share our family recipes with our customers and see the joy in their eyes and on their faces after taking that first bite of the best pulled pork and brisket in the world!" That seems a simple exercise, but it usually takes a while to work through and a couple more times asking why.

A *mind map* puts a topic on the center of a whiteboard or piece of paper, and then creates branches off that topic with related areas. It is usually used in strategic planning to find strategies to achieve a goal. The goal is placed in the middle, and you might list ten or more strategies to achieve the goal. Then you take the top three strategies that will have the most impact.

It may help if you look backward before you look forward. Looking back at your life—including all the critical points in time that added value—will give you a sense of where you're heading. When you see your whole life as a training ground for your ultimate purpose, those experiences will begin pointing you in a direction that makes sense.

After looking back and plotting those experiences, now ask, "Which way forward from here?" What other experiences or training do you need to move towards your purpose?

I've been laid off or fired at least four times. At each job, I learned a different skill necessary for the next level. Often, I couldn't understand the purpose of the experience until I looked back years later. Instead of viewing those events as a setback, I used them to help launch myself toward my future.

Life coaches often use a tool wherein they have you write your obituary. It may seem morbid, but it helps to get you thinking about your purpose and what you want to accomplish in life. What do you want people to say about you? How do you want to be remembered? Once you have this picture in mind, begin to think about what you need to do next to make that happen. What changes need to be made today to become that person you wrote about?

From these two exercises, write a brief mission statement. Try to limit the statement to fourteen words. That is an arbitrary number, but it will help you use concise, clear language.

Self-Talk

How do you see yourself? What topics and words comprise your inner conversations with yourself? Proverbs 23:7 says, "As a man thinks in his heart, so is he." Be careful how your heart thinks about and talks about yourself. If you wouldn't let someone else verbally abuse you, don't do it to yourself!

Don't worry if you aren't yet where you want to be as a person. People with vision apply their self-talk towards where they are going, not where they are. You should build yourself up, not tear yourself down.

I know how negative self-talk starts. You begin to echo the words others have spoken about you. Maybe they said you were stupid; perhaps they said you weren't smart enough to make anything of yourself.

Well, maybe they should shut up! Meanwhile, how do you turn off those voices in your head? That's a good question, and I have a trick to help you. Let's suppose I ask you to count to ten inside your head. Then, when you begin counting, I ask you to tell me your name. If you speak your name, what happens to your counting? The counting stops! There's your answer. To stop thinking negatively, you must speak positively—out loud!

What should you speak? When you talk to yourself or others, you should talk about your vision. Where you want to go. Who you want to become. You should also motivate yourself by encouraging yourself. Remind yourself of what it takes to succeed. Remind yourself of the *seven wealth behaviors*. Sometimes self-motivation even comes from reminding yourself how others have failed or how they didn't put in the work.

Some people use pictures for motivation. A high school girlfriend's dad had a picture of himself on the refrigerator from when he weighed over 300 pounds. At that time, he ran every morning for several miles and weighed just over 180 pounds.

Having a vision means you must have mental toughness. This toughness comes from managing what you say to and about yourself.

When I was in junior high and high school, I had severe asthma. I couldn't run or participate in sports that had long periods of running, like basketball. I loved basketball, so that was disappointing.

When I was thirty-five, I started using new medicines that changed my active life. For the first time ever, I ran two miles straight without stopping. This was an accomplishment on two fronts. First, my lungs weren't gasping for air the whole time. Second, even though I was out of shape and my leg muscles, shins, and feet wanted to stop, I powered through and finished. Now, my longest run has been five miles. It's a very slow run, but I can do it.

Running requires mental toughness. Sometimes I would try to bargain with myself during my longer runs: "Hey, you can stop for a few minutes to walk and then start running again." I learned to run by intermingling walking with running. But I had already pushed through on this distance, so I didn't need to walk. My mind was merely negotiating for peace for my body's sake. So the vision in me answered back, "No, I'm finishing what I started!"

Self-talk and mental toughness help keep you focused on your vision.

Momentum

With vision of financial independence, you build momentum. Momentum means that things start to move forward in your life. You push less on the flywheel to keep it spinning. Now, it spins almost on its own.

Momentum comes when you set your sight on a vision and push forward to that mark. Think about when you were a kid learning to ride your bicycle. You looked ahead at where you wanted to ride—maybe to your neighbor's house, or the end of the driveway. As you started pushing on the pedals, the wheels turned slowly. You used most of your strength just to go a few feet. Then, when you built up speed, the wheels required less effort to keep you moving forward.

All of that progress can stop, however, when you make a hard turn or must turn around.

My youngest son had a hard time learning to ride his bike. One, he has a strong aversion to pain. If you fall while riding a bike, there's a big chance that one of the pedals will hit you in the shins or stab you somewhere soft and vulnerable. Second, he kept focusing on the front wheel instead of looking up where he wanted to go. It wasn't until he began looking up that he had success. Looking forward—with a focused vision—allowed the momentum to build.

Momentum drives you to self-confidence. Note that self-confidence isn't a dirty word. It isn't arrogance or pride. It results from trying, failing, improving, trying again, and succeeding.

Self-confidence attracts others. People will see you moving towards your vision and want to help or be a part.

Having a Plan

People will tell you that you must have a plan and *stick* to the plan. I prefer to think of the plan more fluidly.

Honestly, if I had thought I must stick to a plan when I was twenty to twenty-five years old, I would have considered myself a failure. I had plans. I had things written down as my one-year, three-year, and five-year goals. Yet they often changed during that time—mostly because I was still figuring out who I wanted to be. I wanted to be financially independent. I wanted to be a husband and father.

Besides that, how I got there was fluid. As I said before, I had dreams of becoming an evangelist and then a church accountant/chief financial officer. During those times, following the plan wasn't as important as having a plan.

While I get that people want you to have things mapped out, there must be some flexibility for discovery. You must uncover who you are along the way. What strengths and weaknesses do you possess? Then, when you look at all the things you might be good at, you must ask, "Do I like doing this?" Sometimes the answer is no.

I'm good at many things, like cooking or preparing tax returns. But that doesn't mean that I find any joy in them.

Having the flexibility to discover who you want to become makes all the difference. During my early years after college, I was presented with several choices of occupations and specific jobs. Thankfully, I chose the path that gave me the most flexibility, while also meeting my family's needs.

I felt boxed in with the standard nine-to-five job. If working at a grocery store would give me more flexibility than being an entrepreneur and real estate investor, I would have chosen that. But it didn't.

You need to set goals and write them down. But understand that goals may change. Going from accountant to tax accountant to real estate investor and financial advisor wasn't my original plan. But as I grew and gained experience, I adapted my plan.

You also need to stop worrying about what other people do with their lives. I know many accountants who have worked at the same firm for over twenty years. They have slowly increased their salaries, made partner, and now live quite contentedly. That's great for them. But as Dave Ramsey says on his podcast, *The Ramsey Show*, "In order to live like no one else, you have to live like no one else!" (Ramsey 2018).

Having a vision for financial independence and true wealth means that you must live like no one else. You must make choices based on what will make your vision a reality, not on what is easy or expected. And your goals may change as you gain positive and negative experiences, which teach you lessons and guide you towards your next mark.

Skills and Capabilities

If you still want to move in a direction where you lack the skills, take the time to gain those capabilities.

I've heard young people complain about taking time out of their lives for school. Some think that four years to earn a degree or two to eight years to learn a trade is a long time.

Let's take a moment to gain some perspective. The average person works thirty to fifty years. What percentage of time is four years out of fifty? I'll save you the math; it's 8 percent. If you take time to gain the skills necessary to enter a profession or work in a trade, your annual earnings could increase by 30–80 percent. So, four years of scraping by—compared to forty-six years of earning 30–80 percent more—seems like a pretty good trade-off, doesn't it?

If you don't go into debt, take the time to learn the skills. We will talk about a lifetime of learning in chapter 5.

Your goals may require an investment up front to jump-start your career. Do whatever it takes to make that investment debt-free. (Again, we will discuss avoiding debt in several places in this book. This is the first obstacle you may need to overcome to follow the *seven wealth behaviors*.)

Student debt today is out of control. While I do not believe that the government should just forgive all student loans, it is a problem—especially for people, young and old, who pay for unmarketable degrees. Guaranteed student loans cause tuition costs to keep rising, and colleges to offer degrees which they know will bring no job prospects. They sell a product people want which everyone can pay for—but only with debt. Shouldn't a consumer of education select a degree that will result in a job that pays a competitive wage? Yet if the universities get paid, their attitude may be, *who cares?* It's up to the consumer to understand their own income potential and any loan products offered.

Unfortunately, I used student loans. I probably could have done things differently to avoid them, but I didn't. Fortunately, I did show enough wisdom to choose a degree that was in high demand. Also, I limited my student loans to only what I needed, instead of maxing out the allowed loans. When I graduated, I had less than $20,000 in student loans. Quickly, I made efforts to pay them off. Within a few years, and after flipping a few houses, my student loans were paid off.

Too many high schools lie to kids. They tell them they must go to college to have a promising career. Yet many millionaires who I know work in trades or jobs that don't require a college degree.

Trade schools offer a path to learn a new marketable skill, often while receiving a paycheck. Likewise, apprenticeships and on-the-job training help you learn skills and capabilities while receiving compensation. Some of these jobs require some class time, but most of the learning comes on the job.

My son, Ian, was in class one day when the teacher told the students that they needed a college degree to be successful. My son argued otherwise. Frustrated with his response, the teacher claimed that having a degree was necessary to get a good job.

Ian answered back, "Do you know William Brandt?"

She said, "Yes."

"He is a multi-millionaire with the largest used car dealership in West Texas. He doesn't have a college degree," he replied.

My kids grew up with the Brandts. William Brandt, an actual cowboy from Lakeview, Texas, told me he stumbled into a line of credit and relationships with all the used car managers for new car dealerships right after high school. From that point, he built a small "buy-here, pay-here" used car dealership empire.

When Ian got home from school, we talked about the encounter. Ian said he had asked the teacher if she was successful. Was she a millionaire? Was she wealthy or successful according to our definitions? No, she wasn't. Yet she had followed the path she was encouraging all her students to follow. More than likely, she pays a bunch of student loan debt and lives paycheck to paycheck.

This is not to discredit teachers, but simply to let you know that what you learned in school might not be the only (or best) way to success. Maybe you should go to college, but you shouldn't discount on-the-job training or trade schools.

Having a vision for your life—where it is now and where you want to be—will make the difference in how you live, including the choices you make. That leads us to the next wealth behavior: discipline.

Chapter Summary: The Focus of Vision

- Vision gives your life purpose. When you see into the future and decide what your future will look like, you begin to move in that direction.
- Dreams don't need to be fantastic to spark vision. The dream starts the process that leads you to your vision.
- Your vision should include three intersecting circles: mission, values, and goals.
- Your mission is a simple yet defining statement that sets the boundaries for your decisions toward that purpose.
- Write a brief mission statement. Try to limit the statement to fourteen words—an arbitrary number, but it will help you use concise, clear language.
- People with vision manage their self-talk based on where they are going, not where they are.
- When you talk to yourself or others, you should talk about your vision: where you want to go, who you want to become. You should also motivate yourself by encouraging yourself.
- You should have a plan. However, there must be some flexibility for discovery along the way of who you are.
- You need to set goals and write them down. But understand that goals may change.
- If you still want to move in a direction where you lack the skills, take the time to gain those capabilities.
- Your goals may require an investment up front to jumpstart your career.

CHAPTER 4

THE BRIDGE OF DISCIPLINE

*"A little sleep, a little slumber, a little folding of
the hands to rest; So shall your poverty come like
a prowler and your need like an armed man."*
—Proverbs 24:33-34

Discipline is a four-letter word for many people. They hate it.

My wife is one of those people. Don't get me wrong; she is one of the hardest-working people I know. She just hates the discipline of alarm clocks, schedules, and making plans.

My son-in-law, Ryan, had a hard time with our lack of scheduling when he started dating my daughter. He and his family would schedule vacations and family get-togethers weeks in advance. Whereas our family pretty much would fly by the seat of our pants in social meetups, vacations, and family dinners. Neither method is wrong, but the two approaches to relationships can cause trouble.

A few years ago, we decided to move to another town after months of thought and agonizing about disrupting our kids' lives. Once the decision was made, we moved in two weeks. Other families would have taken a month or two to plan before doing such a thing.

Ryan would get so disheveled when we asked them to go out to eat with us a few minutes before. He wanted to go, but he had a schedule; it would mess with his workout or study time. He is so like me before I was married.

Before I married Angela, I scheduled everything. I was up at 6:30 a.m. every day, reading and praying, then I would work around the house a few minutes before going to work. A week or two into married life, and my scheduled life was all blown to hell.

My wife and I make a good team. Like in *The Matrix*, my job is to balance the equation, and her job is to unbalance it.

Don't confuse discipline with legalism. Legalism steals the joy out of your life and doesn't allow for spontaneity. Discipline, as we will discuss further, has a purpose but allows you the freedom to enjoy relationships and your life.

The Bridge to Your Dreams

A while back, I heard a sermon on discipline that stuck with me all these years. The pastor said, "First there is desire, then discipline, and finally delight." The pastor communicated that discipline is the bridge that brings together *knowing* what you want and *enjoying* what you want.

For example, you might want to play an instrument. You have the desire. The "want to" has been planted as a seed. You think that you might enjoy playing the piano, so you take lessons with a competent piano teacher. After a few weeks, you hate the piano, you hate piano lessons, and most importantly, you hate piano practice. You need discipline to keep going. Discipline will bring you from where you started to enjoying the results.

For those like my wife, who hated any form of discipline completely (she actually hates legalism), you can learn to love discipline and its benefits. Many don't understand discipline. They don't know it brings freedom instead of bondage.

When I was in college, every minute of my day was scheduled. I took eighteen hours of classes and worked a full-time job. In addition, I was a husband and father. My schedule gave me the freedom to enjoy spending time with my wife and daughter instead of worrying about my homework. Since I scheduled my time, I knew I had adequately blocked off time to get to my homework or studying.

We'll talk more about time management later, but what is critical here is that discipline isn't meant to be a burden, but a bridge.

Focused on Vision

For discipline to be effective, you must have a vision. There must be a purpose for the discipline. You need something to look forward to in order to go through the pain of the discipline process. It works in sports, business, and in your personal life. If you don't have a vision, you won't put in the effort.

In addition, you must see results along the way. Discipline in the context of true wealth will not last if you don't begin to see results.

That is why Dave Ramsey's *baby steps* have helped so many people get disciplined in their finances over the years. He gives his followers small success points along the way towards their ultimate goal of being debt-free. With each *baby step*, the person feels some relief from the pressures created by their chaotic financial situation (Ramsey 2022).

The remaining wealth behaviors in this book require discipline. Discipline can be defined and measured by your ability to maintain consistency, constancy, and patience. Let's clarify what a disciplined lifestyle looks like.

Consistency

Consistency is holding to the same process and same routines each and every day. For those seeking true wealth, consistency helps you create habits that reinforce your plans and goals. Consistency repeats motions that help you spin the flywheel of momentum.

Through these patterns of behavior, you build your character. You measure your consistency by whether or not you meet the expectations of yourself and those around you. Can they count on you? Are you trustworthy?

In James Clear's book, *Atomic Habits: Tiny Changes, Remarkable Results*, the author describes how small changes each day done consistently lead to habits that accomplish great results. He shares that if you improve by 1 percent each day, you will improve by thirty-seven times in one year (Clear 2018). That's an amazing outcome by an almost unnoticeable daily act.

How can you change your life by doing one daily act consistently? How would that change your weight? Your health? Your knowledge?

Tucker Max, a five-time *New York Times* bestseller list author, says you should write 250 words per day. With a small word count goal, the likelihood of you completing that goal increases, which then increases the likelihood of you completing your book (Max 2021).

Constancy

Constancy is like *consistency*—not measured by what you do, but by the predictability of your character.

Constancy identifies your position more than your process. Like in math, the constant in the equation never changes. Constancy is who you are on the inside.

Consistency is the result of a constant person's ability to stay strong. It's like a levy that holds firm against the waves of the sea, breaking against it every day. Similarly, a disciplined wealth builder chooses to focus on the goal rather than let their emotions move them out of position.

When I was living with one of my pastors in my early twenties, he set up a few chores for me to do around the house. My examples of family life prior to this had been from a dysfunctional and abusive family that ended in divorce, anger, and bitterness. I chose to submit myself to this training program by my pastor, because I wanted to learn how to be a good future husband and father. I didn't want my past experience to carry forward with my future wife and kids.

In addition, I was in training for the ministry. At the time, I believed that I would be an evangelist or something like that, as I mentioned.

One evening after dinner, I was supposed to wash and put away the dishes. Instead, I had made plans to do "ministry" on the streets of downtown San Marcos, Texas. So, right after dinner, I ran out and went with one of the other young adults in the church. When I got back, no one said anything. The dishes were done and put away, so I went to bed.

The next morning, the pastor called me into his office. He let me know how disappointed he was that I had not kept my word. He said that I owed his wife an apology as well, since she had done what was my responsibility.

While he was talking, I thought, *I don't have to put up with this. I could leave and find work, living with my mother without any chores.*

It was then that I recognized my pattern. Whenever things got difficult, I would cut and run. Instead of being responsible for my actions, I would blame everyone else and take off.

I did apologize to his wife. Then I cleaned their whole house. For the remainder of my time there, I didn't miss one chore. I became a person of my word and backed it up by my consistency and constancy. It was important that others could count on me; that I was trustworthy and faithful.

Patience

Wealth-building takes time and some healthy amounts of patience. True wealth comes from a lifetime spent walking in the *seven wealth behaviors*, not from get-rich-quick schemes. In fact, most get-rich-quick ideas are a sure-fire way to go broke. Most of today's millionaires became wealthy by investing in their company's 401k (or a similar investment option) over a twenty-to-thirty-year period. Those millionaires include trade business owners, self-employed service professionals, and employees who consistently make the maximum contributions to their retirement plans.

You probably didn't want to hear that, but it's true. Wealth takes time to build. Some of that time requires you to wait to purchase things. That's right, wealth-building patiently waits until you have the cash to buy what you want or need. When you are impatient and buy now, pay later, you end up paying for that thing—the object of your desire—plus interest. In contrast, those who have this discipline will see their wealth multiply over time.

Patience and faith together are powerful tools in finding true wealth. Because you believe that your disciplined thoughts and actions will result in financial independence, you can wait for what you want.

I went to work for an accounting firm in Dallas, Texas, in 2001. While filling out the application online, they asked about my salary requirements. I struggled with answering this question, because I didn't live in the metroplex and wasn't sure about the cost of living. I asked my step-grandfather about it, since he had worked for the same company years before.

He said, "Don't worry about the money. Take the job, do your best, and the money will come." That short phrase helped me build wealth through faith and patience.

Building wealth isn't a process that is focused on building wealth. Yes, you read that correctly. It is instead a process focused on *becoming who you were meant to be.* You have a plan to achieve goals; great. Focus on those goals and be the best version of yourself. With faith and patience, the money will come!

Time Management

Discipline involves managing your time well.

You have probably heard the phrase, "You make time for what is important!" The truth is that nobody can make time. Time passes at the same rate, continuously—every second of every day.

And time allows for no do-overs. You can't go back and fix your mistakes or stop time from moving forward. All you can do is make the best use of your time as it passes.

Making the best use of your time begins with a time audit. For two to three weeks, write down everything you do and how much time you spend on each activity. Be honest about how your time was spent. Fibbing here only hurts you.

Now that you have your time audit, ask yourself if the way you spend your time reflects your priorities. Do you see waste in areas of your day or week?

The seven areas of waste, as used in manufacturing, identify ways to improve efficiency in the manufacturing process (EKU 2020). You can also apply them to just about any area of work, time management, or your personal life, asking yourself: *am I allowing any of the seven areas of waste into my week?* We will discuss each of the seven areas of waste and how they apply to wealth-building.

The first area of waste is *waiting*. Are you spending too much time waiting for others, or waiting for things to happen before you can start your tasks? How can you eliminate some of that waiting? Is there some pre-planning you can do to shorten those wait times?

One of my pet peeves is procrastination. Procrastination waits until the last minute to start a project or make a phone call.

In *The Seven Levels of Communication: Go From Relationships to Referrals*, Michael J. Maher encourages us to say, "Do it now!" forty-nine times every day (Maher 2016). As a tool, it battles the urge everyone has to procrastinate. Try it for a week, and see what happens to your activity level.

Over-production is doing too much, or something that someone else could or should do. Can you not get anything done because you're always doing other people's jobs? Or do you have a habit of doing tasks that could be delegated to others?

I asked our executive director of operations to have our podcasts edited. She immediately planned to take it on herself. I knew she would, so I looked up a company that did podcast editing for a reasonable price and forwarded her the link. It was still her responsibility, yet she didn't need to do the work herself. She delegated it to another person or company.

The next area of waste is called *rejects*. This requires you to re-do work. Have you heard the saying, "It's better to do something right the first time than to have to do it over again"? That speaks to the waste of rejects or poor-quality work.

For your personal life, it may mean that you're behaving in a way that created fear or resentment in the past with your relationships. You haven't tried to improve your behavior and keep getting rejected by friends or loved ones.

Once you become aware of the wrong behavior, you can then create new patterns of behavior. Make an effort to change. Recognize this as a timewaster. Your friends and family will notice and deserve better.

In building wealth, you may fail from time to time and have to start over. That's okay—as long as you learn from that failure, become aware of what needs to change, and try to do better.

Excess motion wastes time when you work harder rather than smarter. Is there a better way of doing things? Is there a better route to work? You might ask if there's a better use of your time in your personal life. For example, are you going shopping for supplies rather than ordering them online?

When I was a new business owner, I did all the supply shopping. Unfortunately, I enjoyed looking through clearance at the office supply store too much. If I didn't waste money on clearance items, I know I wasted time. I had to find an alternative, so we found a supplier that was less expensive and shipped the next day. I was also able to delegate that process to my assistant, so that I could spend time with client projects.

Over-processing is the act of working on a project more than is required. It is the paralysis-by-analysis syndrome. Not a real syndrome, but it is a problem. For example, you may analyze investments and fail to ever invest in your pursuit of true wealth.

I had this issue for a while. Before investing in real estate, I bothered my realtor (also the missions pastor at our church) for months and months, asking questions about buying and renting single-family homes. Finally, he looked at me and said, "Brandon, at some point, you're going to have to pull the trigger and buy a house!" He was right. I over-processed all the information I thought I needed before I could buy my first rental. So I bought my first house, which led to us buying more than one hundred single-family homes.

Excess inventory can mean many things in the area of time management. Either you're spending too much time on something unproductive, or you're filling your schedule with non-priority activities. Sometimes the unproductive but necessary items can be automated. You might be able to use an app or hire someone to take those items off your plate. Technology today can improve your time management skills.

Your calendar, banking apps, phone, and home computer can all help you automate some activities and free up time. I now use a calendar app, whereby I send a link to people who would like to meet with me during the week. Instead of sending emails back and forth until we have an agreed-upon date, they choose a slot I have allocated for those meetings.

Finally, *transportation* is the last of the seven wastes. Transportation in the context of time management might mean eliminating the time required to move back and forth between tasks—like using Zoom instead of holding a face-to-face meeting. Leaving your office to go and physically meet with a vendor or client takes time in traffic getting there, sitting in a waiting room, and driving home. Also, addressing this time waste could include choosing to fly to a conference instead of drive. It may also involve sending an email instead of scheduling a meeting.

Once you have identified the wastes in your current schedule from your time audit diary, you can create your *stop-doing list*. Every January, people start the year with their new year's resolutions. Those are usually a list of things they will do or complete by the end of the year. Equally important—and critical to your time management—is your stop-doing list. What things will you eliminate from your life? You don't have to wait until the new year to make this list. Also, it probably should be reviewed regularly throughout the year.

Next, determine how to *time block* your perfect week. When do you want to work on your priority tasks? Mornings, afternoons, evenings? Set appointments with yourself for those tasks.

Are some of your priorities not in your schedule at all? In order to ensure they happen, insert them. For example, I have a set appointment two times a week for martial arts training. Yes, it's right in the middle of the day, but I need that time to be a better executive, manager, and employee. This activity recharges me for the rest of the week—a week which sometimes drains me.

I also have two appointments with myself per week wherein I schedule nothing. I just think. They aren't long appointments, but they are crucial.

Do you have a block for exercise? Thinking? Time with your spouse? Time with God? Whatever you say your priorities are, prove it by setting appointments for them. And then protect those times!

Following these steps won't solve all your problems, but doing so will help you manage them better. Remember, they call this "time management." That's because your time must be managed. You may need to go through this exercise at least once a year, maybe more.

I heard a business advisor say that he looks at all of his responsibilities at the beginning of each year. Then he delegates half of those activities to others to free his time for new activities. I'm not sure I would go that far, but you may find through examining your activities that half of what you're doing is unnecessary. Allocate time to your priorities. If you get rid of half your activities, that's more time for you, your spouse, and your kids!

Start small—by delegating and assigning tasks to your stop-doing list. The more you go through this process, the easier it will become. It's like moving; you never know how much junk you own until it's time to move. Don't wait until moving day to purge the clutter.

From the discussion in this chapter, you should see that the behavior of discipline consists of a set of supporting practices. You may be great at some things but still need to work on others. That's okay. We're all a work in process. Having faith and patience, being constant, acting consistently, and managing your time moves you closer to your goal of financial independence.

As we've explored, vision is necessary for discipline to be effective. Discipline is necessary to incorporate the remaining wealth behaviors into your life.

Note that you are never at a place where discipline won't be essential for financial independence. When you hear of someone wealthy who lost everything, their decline probably started with a lapse of discipline.

Next, we will talk about how wealth-builders read and consume information, as we explore developing a lifestyle of learning.

Chapter Summary: The Bridge of Discipline

- First, there is desire, then discipline, and finally delight. Discipline is the bridge that brings together *knowing what you want* and *enjoying what you want.*
- Discipline brings freedom instead of bondage.
- For discipline to be effective, you must have a vision—including a purpose for the discipline. You need something to look forward to in order to go through the pain of the discipline process.
- Consistency is holding to the same process and routines each and every day.
- Consistency is measured by whether you meet your expectations of yourself and those around you. Can they count on you? Are you trustworthy?
- Constancy is like consistency—however not in the processes you work, but in what you believe and who you are.
- Constancy is who you are on the inside. Consistency is the result of a constant person's ability to stay strong.
- Wealth-building takes time and healthy amounts of patience. True wealth comes from a lifetime spent walking in the *seven wealth behaviors,* not from get-rich-quick schemes.
- Patience and faith together are powerful tools in finding true wealth.
- Discipline involves managing your time well. Making the best use of your time begins with a time audit.

- The seven areas of waste used in manufacturing identify ways to improve efficiency in the manufacturing process. They also can be applied to just about any area of work, time management, or life.
- Once you have identified the wastes in your current schedule from your time audit, you can create your *stop-doing list*.
- Next, *time block* your weekly schedule to work on your priority tasks. Set appointments with yourself for those tasks. Whatever you say your priorities are, prove it by setting appointments for them. Then protect those times!

CHAPTER 5

THE LIFESTYLE OF LEARNING

*"Take firm hold of instruction, do not let
go; Keep her, for she is your life."*
—Proverbs 4:13

Early in my daughter's education, she struggled with reading. In the first and second grades, she wasn't developing her reading skills like the other kids were.

God forgive me and any parent who compares the development of their kid to that of the "other kids." Yet we were new parents, so we didn't have any experience with educating our kids or knowing what pace to expect our daughter to develop. In addition, my wife had some terrible private school education experiences with teachers and administrators who had no business teaching.

Angela, my wife, didn't trust teachers, and I was ignorant of early childhood development. So, I listened quietly while the teachers stated that Kate, my daughter, more than likely had some learning disabilities.

My wife's reaction was to steam quietly as the teacher spoke. Then when we got home—or more accurately, on the way there—she rebuked that teacher and "cursed her words." That is religious-speak for vehemently disagreeing with the teacher's assessment.

We kept Kate at that school until the end of the school year, then had to decide where she would go the next year. To allow her to develop her reading skills, we decided to have her repeat the second grade. She still might be a bit angry with us for this choice, but we thought it was best at the time.

The second time through second grade, she had one of the best teachers any of our kids would ever encounter. That teacher told Kate, "You are smart and capable. There is nothing that can hold you back!" During that year, we saw a drastic change in Kate's reading skills. Quickly, she rose to the top of her class and never looked back.

In high school, she was in the top 10 percent of her class with a 4.0 grade-point average. She has read well over fifty books per year since she was a freshman in high school. She loves novels of love, fantasy, and adventure.

The challenge of reading she experienced early pushed her to excel in her reading. Like she has something to prove to the world, she consumes literature as much as she eats or breathes.

As a wealth-builder, you should be like Kate and possess a lifestyle of *learning*. Consume information from those who have been where you want to go. A lifestyle of learning isn't just for your job or occupation, but it should be an attitude and a daily habit. Like I ask my kids when they get home from school, you should ask yourself, "What did I learn today?"

Humility

The lifestyle of learning starts with humility. How can you learn anything else if you believe that you already know everything?

You can say that you don't believe you know everything, but your actions can prove otherwise. If you aren't reading, listening to podcasts, taking courses, or receiving instruction from a mentor or coach, what is your lifestyle saying?

Humility says that *I can learn from anyone and in any circumstance*. The value of humility cannot be understated. Do you choose to learn from your failures? When was the last time you tried something and failed miserably? Did you blame others, or did you reflect on what happened and your role in the failure?

A few years ago, I purchased an accounting book of business from a retiring CPA. It was a complete failure. I had bought a book in the same area the year before and wanted to add to our client base. Regrettably, this firm was utterly incompatible with ours. Their fee structure, process, and the client's expectations of how long the process would take differed from ours.

All of that led to anger and frustration among the clients and my staff. I have told my team on several occasions that the whole thing should never have happened. I didn't do my due diligence in non-financial areas. I didn't consider the conflict that the change in process for the new (to us) clients would create for my staff. I can't apologize enough. Thankfully, my team has forgiven me.

Would they have been so forgiving if I had blamed them for the mess? Or if I went out and did the same thing again? I don't think so. For the wealth-builder, humility causes you to learn from your failures and your victories. It keeps you honest about your decisions and how they affect those around you.

As you move towards financial independence, you will make mistakes. Along the way, take time to reflect on those mistakes and learn from them.

Sources for Continuous Improvement

Now that you have humbly accepted the idea of a lifestyle of learning, where do you start? There are several sources that can support your continuous improvement. Choose learning materials that will challenge you, educate you, and inspire you. These sources include podcasts, blogs, YouTube videos, and books.

Podcasts. An entry point into continuous improvement is the podcast. There are thousands of podcasts on an enumerable number of subjects. These podcasts can be as entertaining as they are educational. For you, as the wealth-builder, I would start with financial podcasts. Maybe even delve into the occasional leadership podcast. My favorite podcasts deal with specialized topics like real estate or asset protection.

You can try the *Rich Dad Radio Show*, the *BiggerPockets Real Estate Podcast*, or *The Fun Money Podcast*, which is hosted by my former intern, CPA-turned-financial-advisor, Ross Powell, and his friend, Josh Hargrove. Also, I have a podcast called *Coaching For Profit*, in which I discuss issues related to entrepreneurs, small business owners, real estate, and money.

People will listen to hours of entertainment podcasts every day. If you're listening to a podcast, why not listen to something that will help make you better? Either better at your job or better at being human? Set a goal to listen to at least two podcasts per week about financial independence, real estate, business, or leadership. Set an annual goal of one hundred podcast episodes. Begin the process of working on you!

Blogs. Blogs are often the rantings of authors on various topics that may or may not help you. However, there are blogs by financial advisors, wealth managers, and real estate investors that can be a "wealth" of information—pun intended. Try www. FinancialSamurai.com to start. I also like www.OneFrugalGirl. com. They both chronicle their journey to financial independence and have different reasons for doing so.

Blogs are great places to glean information on specific topics. They are an excellent source for the person looking for an introduction to the topic. Blogs aren't usually full of research, however, so I wouldn't quote them or make decisions based on what you read there. Most blogs are full of the authors' opinions and should be evaluated appropriately.

If you get turned on by a topic, do your own research and see how you might apply what you have learned to your life. You should set a goal of one to two blogs per month to stay informed and help inspire creativity.

YouTube. Another one of my favorite sources for continuous improvement is YouTube video courses. Any time I want to learn how to do something, and I think you may too, I look it up on YouTube. I have learned how to program my garage door, replace the filter on my water softener, and play a specific part of a song on the piano from watching YouTube videos. There are countless how-to videos on YouTube for an enumerable number of tasks.

Did you know there are also YouTube channels for how to write a novel, invest in real estate, create a balanced portfolio, and create a budget for your family? Later, I will talk about one of my favorite YouTube channels, where a man teaches young people how to do things usually passed down from dad to son or daughter.

Books. One of the benefits of listening to podcasts and watching YouTube video courses is finding out the best books to read. Another source of continuous improvement, reading books gives you an in-depth picture of the author's expertise and experience. I recommend reading between twenty to thirty books per year.

I have been on a journey over the last decade to change how I interact with others. That journey began by reading books on relationships, psychology, team building, and leadership. I have been an introverted, arrogant, condescending asshole for most of my teens to mid-thirties. I became aware of my short-comings and wanted to figure out why and how to repair my relationships.

Set a goal for yourself. If you aren't a fast reader like me, use audiobooks to train your reading pace. You can set the speed of the narration to whatever you're comfortable with. I prefer listening at 1.25 to 1.5 times the regular rate. Some folks will listen at 2 times the standard speed, but they're just crazy! I don't know how you get anything from the book (or podcast) at that speed. But I'm sure your amazing mind will adjust to the speed, and it will sound normal after a while.

As a CPA, financial advisor, and entrepreneur, I have spent most of my time reading business books. Those are great, and you should read them too if you are an entrepreneur. However, what is the point if you gain the whole world yet lose your soul? My friends and family deserved better. I needed to become a better man, husband, and father. Because of this, I chose to read books like *Integrity: The Courage to Meet the Demands of Reality* and *Necessary Endings: The Employees, Businesses, and Relationships That All of Us Have to Give Up to Move Forward* by Dr. Henry Cloud. Also, *The Four Laws of Love: Guaranteed Success for Every Married Couple* by Jimmy Evans, *Developing the Leader Within You* by John C. Maxwell, and many, many more. I'm still on that journey. My kids and wife will tell you it's working.

Coaches and Mentors

The Mentor. Coaches and mentors are not the same. A coach can train you in your desired skills and guide you toward your desired outcome. A mentor has done what you want to do. A mentor can be a coach, but not all coaches can be considered mentors.

Mentors bring the value of their experience to the table. Having a mentor is vital in the early stages of growth. When you begin your journey towards financial independence, you need to be inspired, and you need someone who can show you the way. The mentor does both.

How do you find a mentor? That's a good question. A mentor for wealth might not be in your inner circle. You may need look outside your typical acquaintances to find someone who has true wealth. Remember not to be fooled by the new-money-rich folks with high incomes and very little net worth. It may take some investigation on your part to find someone living in quiet wealth. The signs should be someone who lives below their means, only pays cash for things they want, and dresses and acts modestly. Reference *The Millionaire Next Door* by Thomas Stanley for a more detailed description of the truly wealthy.

When you find someone, see about getting an introduction. Last year, I heard about a real estate investor near us who spent his life raising capital for large office, multi-family, and industrial properties. Through a few networking and church events, I met someone who worked for him. They offered to introduce us, and I accepted. When we met on the phone for the first time, he seemed surprised that I wanted to meet. I had told him of my experience in single-family homes, but I was interested in learning about multi-family properties. I knew that I couldn't get there without a mentor like him. He agreed to an in-person meeting the following week.

I have had other mentors. In my book *The E-Hero's Guide to Real Estate Investing: Increase Your Cash Flow Without Increasing Your Work Day,* I discussed the value of a mentor. I talked about my first mentor, Pastor Darrel, the Indiana Jones of mission work. He had owned twenty-six properties or more, and I hadn't yet bought my first. Then, when I had gathered more than twenty properties, I looked to another mentor, Max Jacobs. He and his partner owned more than one hundred houses (or "doors," as they say in the industry). With his experience and insight, I grew my portfolio to over one hundred houses.

When you approach a potential mentor to secure great advice, you should value their time, appreciate their advice, and do something with it.

Ask for an appointment or a few minutes on the phone in your first contact with your mentor. When you set the appointment for thirty minutes, end it before the thirty-minute mark. If you value their time, they will be more likely to give you more later if you ask.

Always show your gratitude. Say "thank you" for their advice and time. If they can't make an appointment, thank them for letting you know and ask to reschedule. The potential mentor isn't blowing you off. Rather, they are probably swamped with responsibilities. Respect that and be gracious.

Finally, do something! It's not enough to ask for advice. You must show that you're using the advice you receive. Otherwise, you're telling your mentor that their advice doesn't have value. This wastes their time, which breaks the first rule of approaching a mentor.

The Coach. Although very similar to mentoring, a coach doesn't necessarily have any experience in the area they coach. "What?!" you may gasp. But a coach is still helpful in guiding your development by asking questions that promote active learning. Coaching is part of a continuous improvement strategic plan. The coach enables you to determine where you are *now, where* you want to be, and *how* you will get there. I call this the *now, where, how strategic planning method.* This was adapted by concepts from Dr. Chris Mason, founder of Mindshop, a company devoted to empowering others with tools and training in business advisory (Mindshop 2021).

For coaching to work well, the advisor should draw on the expertise and understanding of the coachee. By using workshops, tools, compelling questions, and active listening, the coach guides you to reach your next level of success, overcome obstacles that get in the way, and stay on pace towards your goals. Our firm has been coaching business owners for years. Financial coaching may be what you need to reach your goal of financial independence.

I recently coached a young couple about their financial well-being. They had accumulated an excessive amount of consumer debt. They had some decisions to make about whether to sell a vacant lot and pay down their consumer debt. Since my role as a coach forbids me to tell them exactly what to do, I referred to their goals. They had written out several goals with a timeline of ten years. As I began reading their goals, reminding them of their vision of financial independence, they agreed to sell the lot with a value of more than half of their consumer debt. It wasn't an easy decision, but I believe (and they believed) that it was the right decision.

Coaching helps the coachee to activate natural learning as well. Natural learning occurs when you become self-aware of issues and behavior. If that behavior is negative, you can then make changes to avoid engaging in it again. If it's positive, being self-aware allows you to focus and reinforce that behavior.

For example, I used to have a short temper. I can remember my parents, brother, and cousins calling me "little hulk"—not because I looked like Lou Ferrigno, but because of my anger issues. I would lose my temper repeatedly and explode into a rage. Later, I learned to suppress the anger, yet it didn't disappear.

In my late thirties, I became aware that fear triggered most of my anger. Even though I didn't blow up, curse, or break things anymore, I still felt the heat and inner turmoil of that rage. I understood that I was responding to the fear of things not going my way. Or I was demanding what I wanted by focusing that fear into rage against that person or thing. Now, I reassure myself that whatever happened to trigger the anger only distracts from my purpose. I choose not to take it personally and then choose to find a solution.

Having a financial coach can help you accelerate becoming self-aware of behaviors and issues. As they work with you to respond to your life issues, they will see patterns of behavior and can address them. Although this can happen only if you are humble and willing to let them help.

Activation

Activation begins when you apply what you have learned. We already touched on this when we discussed that if you don't take the mentor's advice, you tell the mentor that you don't value that advice. It's not enough to feed your mind with facts and information. That information must move to the next level, where information becomes knowledge. Knowledge comes from experience with information.

While working as an associate pastor, we believed that there were three parts to the worship service: worship, the Word, and prayer.

Of course, the worship team would lead the congregation in singing songs and hymns—praising God. This part of the service prepared people's hearts to hear God.

The next part of the service was the Word—preaching, or teaching the Bible. The congregation would listen to instruction from the Bible (hopefully from the Bible!), and somehow the pastor/preacher/teacher would apply the Word of God to listeners' lives. This teaching of the Word often included three points, supported by Scripture and illustrated by stories, poems, or humorous anecdotes.

I know you're saying, "Get to the point, Brandon!" All that has transpired up to this point has been learning about and giving worship to God. Some churches and many churchgoers stop the process at this point.

Yet the service should lead to the final part of *activation*. How will you apply what you have learned today? In some churches, the pastor may ask, "What is the Holy Spirit saying to you?" They want you to connect with God's Word through action. And that is what turns information into knowledge.

When you have gone beyond just reading that a process works, but rather have experienced it with your senses, you no longer have mere book learning. You know it. Activation bridges between the two. It says, "This is the way! I have experienced it for myself!"

Activation is great, but the next wealth behavior goes even further.

Chapter Summary: The Lifestyle of Learning

- As a wealth builder, you should have a lifestyle of *learning*. Consume information from those who have been where you want to be. The lifestyle of learning should be in your attitude and be a daily habit.
- The lifestyle of learning starts with humility. How can you learn if you believe that you know everything?
- Reading, listening to podcasts, taking courses, or receiving instruction from a mentor or coach communicates humility and a desire to learn.
- Set goals for yourself: How many books per year will you read? How many podcasts per week will you listen to? How many blogs or YouTube videos/courses will you learn from per month?
- A mentor is someone who has done what you want to do.
- When you approach a potential mentor to get great advice, you should value their time, appreciate their advice, and do something with it.
- Although very similar to mentoring, coaching doesn't require that the coach have any experience in their coaching area.
- A coach enables you to determine where you are now, where you want to be, and how you will get there.
- Coaching helps the coachee to activate natural learning. Natural learning occurs when you become self-aware of issues and behavior.

- Activation begins when you apply what you have learned.
- Don't just feed your mind with facts; move to the next level by mixing that information with experience. The result is knowledge.

CHAPTER 6

THE VALUE OF WISDOM

"Happy is the man who finds wisdom, and the man who gains understanding; For her proceeds are better than the profits of silver, and her gain than fine gold."
—Proverbs 3:13–14

When I was a kid, I remember hearing the story of Solomon in the Bible—how he was asked by God what he wanted. God would have given him anything he asked for, but because Solomon asked for wisdom, God gave him riches and wealth as well.

Of course, because I wanted to be wealthy, I also asked God for wisdom. I'm not sure what I was expecting to happen then. Maybe a cloud developing inside of our house, a hand reaching through the cloud towards my head, and as it touched me, all the world's secrets being revealed?

In truth, not much happened with Solomon either. God said yes, then Solomon went about his business.

The value of *wisdom* as a wealth behavior will set you apart from those around you.

Wisdom and Wealth

Before we define wisdom, let's think about where it comes from. Or more specific, when it comes.

It should be noted that wisdom and wealth go hand in hand. When I think about the story of king Solomon now, I wonder if the desire for wisdom brings about wisdom. Proverbs says that "wisdom cries out from the highest places of the city, whoever is simple, let him turn in here" (Proverbs 9:3–4). But it also says that foolishness calls out too (Proverbs 9:14–16).

It's a choice that everyone must make; you must choose the path of wisdom. Which direction will you go?

Why does wealth seem to follow wisdom? Obviously, if wealth came first, without wisdom, it wouldn't last very long. Or maybe no one looks for wisdom where poverty and lack abound? For example, would you take financial advice from your uncle, who lives paycheck to paycheck in that mobile home park?

True wealth follows a life led by wisdom. Usually, you obtain wealth through disciplined actions that lead to your success.

You can see how certain behaviors contribute to your wealth, where other behaviors detract from it. When you begin to accumulate wealth, others notice and want to learn how you did it. That's why there are tons of "how-to" videos on Facebook and YouTube. Someone figured something out (with wisdom) and wants to share it with the world. That's awesome! I even have a YouTube channel for our firm with podcasts and, in the future, instructional videos on real estate investing, wealth building, and being an entrepreneur.

The information is out there. Do you have the discipline, faith, and patience to walk out the seven wealth behaviors to see it through? Like I said before, the behaviors are not a secret, nor are they complex. Yet they *are* challenging to put into practice.

What Is Wisdom?

Wisdom not only acts on what you learn, through activation, but decides the best actions to take. Wisdom isn't super-spiritual or some ancient code to crack.

The dictionary defines wisdom as *the ability to discern inner qualities and relationships; insight; good sense.* That doesn't really help me. Does it help you? To me, that doesn't allow me to determine whether I have it.

I don't remember what book I read, but some ancient philosopher, maybe Socrates, said wisdom knows that you don't know anything. I'm not sure that helps either, because I know some things. By that definition, I guess I would not be wise.

So, how do you know a wise person when you see one? You don't, at least not initially. You see the results of their actions. A person must have a consistent stream of positive results to be considered wise. Instead of determining what wisdom is, consider looking at what wisdom does.

So, what does wisdom do? Wisdom makes good choices, comprehends the seasons of life, and understands people. Let's explore a bit to better understand those three areas.

Making Good Choices

As a kid, I can't say that I made good choices. In fact, from ages thirteen to nineteen, most of my decisions were selfish and self-destructive. One of my patterns of decisions included running away when things got hard or didn't go my way. In fact, I ran away from home when I was sixteen.

This was a stupid decision, but that doesn't mean I didn't feel justified. My dad was constantly berating me about my shortcomings. Nothing I did was ever good enough. I spent most of my time around him just hoping he would ignore me, so he wouldn't lose his temper and verbally accost me.

On this day, my dad and I had a big fight over something ridiculous, which pushed me over the edge. I went into the basement and found a duffle bag. I shoved clothes, underwear, and shoes into that bag, grabbed a few other things from my bedroom, and took off in my 1978 Pontiac Grand Prix.

Only it wasn't my car. It was in my dad's name.

I went to a friend's dorm room at the University of Central Missouri. If I remember right, it was a Saturday, so we spent the day getting wasted. Sunday, we did the same thing. There weren't cell phones at the time, so I had no contact with my dad. (I'm not sure what thoughts filled his head; we never talked about it after or since.)

That Monday, after taking a quick paper towel bath in the McDonald's bathroom sink, I went to school. What would you do have done? I didn't have any problems at school. I just hated being around my family.

As I left school with my girlfriend, a police officer pulled me over. They had waited for me at the end of the school driveway. Since I hadn't turned seventeen yet, I'd broken the law by running away. The whole school watched as the police handcuffed me and put me in the back of their cruiser. My girlfriend had to drive my car home.

The system gave me a probation officer, and I had to check in each week. Had I just waited a month, I could have moved out legally. I'm not sure if that would have been better for me, but I know going home after this episode was the worst. I didn't act wisely when I ran away from home. I couldn't see anything ahead of my current pain.

Making good choices means that you have the judgment and experience to decide. That doesn't mean that you won't make mistakes. It means that you learn from each decision, and especially from your mistakes. You often won't know the right call until after the decision is made. Wisdom comes when you have had enough experiences, or have the judgment to see the consequences behind every choice. Failure only increases your knowledge and understanding for the next decision.

In the game of chess, an experienced player can see the possible outcomes of one, three, or four moves ahead. Consequences follow every decision. Whether positive or negative, you will deal with the results of that decision. Wisdom not only includes assessing the consequences that you might experience, but it also includes realizing the consequences that those around you might experience. These actions and reactions determine the game of life. Shakespeare said, "All the world's a stage, and all the men and women merely players" (*As You Like It, Act 2, Scene 7*) (Shakespeare 1623).

For those seeking financial independence, your choices today will determine your future. A wrong financial decision in your youth can make it more challenging to buy a house, finance a car, or get the job you want. You need wisdom to make good choices that will keep you on the path to financial independence.

Understanding the Seasons of Life

Wisdom helps you understand where you are in life. Periods of intensity follow periods of rest, and then it happens again. This part of wisdom sees that you can endure anything for a season. You can survive a master's program while working fifty hours per week, because it's just a season. You can tolerate learning the ropes at a new job, because this is just a season.

After marrying Angela in April of 1996, I went back to college in January 1998. My first child was born the semester I started back; it was hard. Angela and I agree that it was the most challenging part of our lives. But even then, we knew this too would pass. There was a light at the end of that tunnel. We knew that the hardship we endured would pay off in the future.

Many people do not have this wisdom. They can't see beyond today.

My friend Devin had worked for Taco Bell since high school. They offered him management positions at age nine-teen and almost every year after. He never took the promo-tions, because that would mean working fifty hours a week in-stead of forty. He couldn't see that the promotion was a season to be endured for something greater, yet it could have led to him owning a franchise or two.

If you can't see past your current season in life, you will never have the patience and faith to endure for something greater.

I learned early on why it seems like time takes so much longer while you're young compared to when you're older. As an eighteen-year-old, one year equals one-eighteenth of your life. However, when you are forty years old, one year is one-fortieth of your life. As a ratio of your lifespan, each year is smaller and smaller, thus seeming to take less time each year.

I've talked to many young adults about going to college, a trade school, or something similar. Four years in school seems like such a long time. But in comparison to your working life of almost fifty years, what is four years? It's only 8 percent of your working life. Wisdom understands this and sees through the seasons of life.

To have true wealth, you must be able to see ahead, endure today, and press on. We talked about having a vision as the first wealth behavior. You must keep your eyes on your vision to get to your desired destination, which takes discipline. The wealth behavior of wisdom requires the ability to see the consequences of your financial decisions.

Every cause has an effect. Before making financial decisions, zoom out a bit and look past today. Use a mind map or other tool to brainstorm the possible impact of those decisions. It's better to take the time to walk through the consequences of your choices on a whiteboard rather than having those consequences thrust upon you by surprise.

Understanding People

Understanding people requires empathy. From Wikipedia, empathy is *the capacity to understand or feel what another person experiences from within their frame of reference, that is, the capacity to place oneself in another's position.* Basically, empathy puts you inside the other person's life, in their shoes. What are their fears, dreams, joys, and desires?

I struggle with empathy. As I have stated before, my father is a hard, overbearing, judgmental man. Unfortunately, I have also been judgmental most of my life. I'm still working on showing affection and appreciation to others and understanding them on an individual level.

You (and I) should try to remember three things: hear what the person *feels* more than what they *say*, do to others what you would want others to do to you, and see and appreciate the value in others. In the next few paragraphs, we will discuss each one of these empathy practices.

First, *hearing what others are feeling.* Sometimes what people say has nothing to do with how they feel. Their body language, tone, and facial expressions tell so much more than their words. I have had clients rage against me or someone else and immediately apologize. The rage was because someone they loved died or they lost their job. Some other trauma crashed down on them, and I stood in the way as the innocent bystander in the wrong place at the wrong time.

My pastor used to say, "We judge other people on their actions and ourselves on our intentions." This means if we could know what goes on inside the hearts and minds of the people we come in contact with, we would not be so quick to judge them. Empathy takes the time to ask questions and discover the person behind the fear or anger.

Doing to others what you would want them to do to you is known as the golden rule. Almost all cultures have some form of this commandment. I like how Jesus made it active. The golden rule doesn't wait to see if someone will do something and then do the same in return. Instead, empathy actively looks to treat others with respect or bless them whether or not they reciprocate. Your actions should not depend on others' behavior.

Years ago, my kids and I regularly went to a martial arts school. For seven years, we attended and became a part of that community. The instructor and I became friends, even going to lunch or the shooting range occasionally. Then we had a disagreement about some things, and I decided that we would go to a different school. Often, I met people around town who went to my previous school. When they asked what happened, I purposed never to speak negatively about the instructor.

On the other hand, the instructor did not give me the same courtesy. Yet that doesn't matter. Wisdom says that we do good to others no matter how they behave. I'm not saying you lay down and take a beating, verbally or otherwise. No, I'm saying that you shouldn't let others define your character.

When you choose to do good for others, you will receive good back. It is the law of sowing and reaping, which we will discuss more in chapter 9. There are three keys to the law of sowing and reaping: First, you will reap what you sow, good or bad. Second, you will reap more than you sow. Seeds turn into trees that produce thousands of seeds. Third, you will reap after you sow. Reaping doesn't happen first. Wisdom understands this law. Empathy actively sows good into other people's lives.

Finally, *empathy means that you see the value in others and find a way to appreciate them.* The highest purpose of wisdom is to show appreciation to others and help them become the best version of themselves. Empathy says, "You have value, and I appreciate you."

One of the best books on showing appreciation is *The 5 Languages of Appreciation in the Workplace: Empowering Organizations by Encouraging People*, by Gary Chapman and Paul White. It is based on Gary Chapman's book, *The 5 Love*

Languages: Secrets to Love That Lasts. They describe how we each give and receive appreciation, or love, very differently. The five appreciation languages are *words of affirmation, quality time, acts of service, tangible gifts*, and *physical touch*.

Most people have one or two ways they receive appreciation: one primary and one secondary. If your appreciation language is receiving gifts, but I tend to give appreciation by words of affirmation, you might not feel appreciated. And to truly value someone, you must care enough about them to show your appreciation in a language they understand. Within our firm, I try to show my appreciation using all the languages (except physical touch, when it isn't appropriate or possible).

I admit that I have struggled with showing appreciation to those I value and love. In the last few years, I have been actively working on how I show appreciation, both at home and in the workplace. Last Christmas, when our firm was deciding what raises to give, I selected a few people from our staff and sent them hand-written thank-you cards. In my horrible handwriting, I encouraged each team member on those cards and thanked them for something specific they had done for the firm or me. The feedback I received was very positive—not just for the raises, but also for the notes of appreciation and encouragement.

The *value of wisdom* in wealth-building can't be overstated. Making good choices, understanding the seasons of life, and understanding people all make up the way of the wise.

You should read a chapter of the book of Proverbs in the Bible each day to help you in this behavior. There are thirty-one chapters, so you can read the chapter that coincides with the date.

Next, we will discuss one of the hardest behaviors to master.

Chapter Summary: The Value of Wisdom

- Wisdom and wealth go hand in hand.
- True wealth follows a life lead by wisdom. Usually, you obtain wealth through disciplined actions that lead to your success.
- Wisdom not only acts on what you learn, the activation, but decides the best actions to take?
- Wisdom makes good choices, understands the seasons of life, and understands people.
- Making good choices means that you have the judgment and experience to decide.
- Understanding the seasons of life, wisdom sees that you can endure anything for a season.
- To understand people, remember three things: Hear what the person feels more than what they say, do to others what you would want others to do to you, and see and appreciate the value in others.

CHAPTER 7

THE SACRIFICE OF THRIFT

"Go to the ant, you sluggard! Consider
her ways and be wise,
which having no captain, overseer, or ruler,
provides her supplies in the summer,
and gathers her food in the harvest."
—Proverbs 6:6–8

My first job out of college was working for a CPA named Van Carson. His father who had left him the business had been a CPA as well.

I had heard a bit about his dad when I interviewed with another firm. Apparently, Mr. Carson, Van's father, and two other CPAs had planned to start their own firm when at the last minute, Mr. Carson pulled out. The other two CPAs formed the same firm that was interviewing me. They didn't tell me why Mr. Carson changed his mind, but they asked me, "Does he still use both sides of the calculator tape?"

Now, I hadn't noticed it before, but I suddenly remembered seeing Van roll up his used calculator tape when they asked. Then, it dawned on me that he did that to use the other side of the tape. That exemplified the sacrifice of *thrift*.

In the interview, everyone laughed when I affirmed that he continued to do so. But inside, my respect for Van increased that day. He sometimes struggled in his interactions with people, though he was wealthy.

Thrift is defined as *the quality of using money and other resources carefully and not wastefully.* As one of the seven wealth behaviors, thrift is a philosophy of spending. To be thrifty, you must have a purpose for money beyond your current needs or selfish desires. Thrift tells your money what to do, instead of allowing your bills to dictate what your money will do.

Imagine being able to direct every dollar to a desired end. You wake up each day knowing that your money isn't bleeding from your checking account. It takes direction from you each day to accomplish the task of moving you and your family towards financial independence.

In this chapter, we will discuss this behavior and what it means for you and your family, as well as what derails the sacrifice of thrift.

What Is the Sacrifice of Thrift?

As we mentioned before, thrift is deciding how to spend your money and resources in a way that prepares you for your future. It involves budgeting, saving, staying out of debt, and negotiating good deals.

Being thrifty is a way of life for the wealthy. I once knew a multi-millionaire who spent two hours on the telephone with a utility company arguing over a $37 charge on his invoice. Many millionaires believe that if you take care of the pennies, the dollars will take care of themselves.

This chapter will help you take care of the pennies. Until this point, you have read about non-financial behaviors that will guide you to true wealth. This chapter and the ones that follow deal with dollars and cents.

Comparison

All of us have a hard time with comparison. A few years ago, as my staff and I were painting the walls of our new office building, a man walked in and disturbed our lunch break. He wore clothes that clearly had been slept in and was, overall, a walking mess.

Then he approached me and asked if we were hiring.

Looking confused, I asked, "Hiring for what?"

He said he was a certified public accountant (CPA) and handed me a copy of his resume.

I stopped eating and invited him into our new conference room.

He told me he had been living in a shelter and was an alcoholic. He was trying to get his life back together. He had years of experience, so I took a chance and gave him a job.

Months later, somehow, he found out that I was paying another accountant over $10,000 more per year. He couldn't understand why I would pay him so little when he was a

CPA, and she was not. He requested a meeting and let me know what he discovered; he wanted me to fix it by giving him a raise. He could not let go of the fact that someone without a certificate could make more than him—ignoring the facts that he was being paid more than enough to live comfortably, and that he was no longer homeless. Instead, he chose to obsess over something he had no control over, which didn't affect his wellbeing.

Yet that's what many of us do, especially with social media. People typically only post about the best parts of their lives. Then we obsess over what others have, instead of being content with what we have. We compare ourselves to others in what we wear, where we live, and what we drive.

Comparison poisons the soul of the entitled. We believe that we deserve something that someone else has. We don't know what they have gone through to get those things, nor what they are still going through. We probably don't even care. Yet, we still find a way to covet their lives or possessions.

Those who practice the sacrifice of thrift know that the only comparison we should be making is today versus yesterday.

A leader at a youth camp in Texas would say, "I'm not where I want to be, but thank God I'm not where I used to be!" The good kind of comparison tracks your progress. It compares your current net worth, monthly cash flow from investments, relationships with your family, and leadership development, not to others but to where you were one, three, or five years ago. This wealth behavior doesn't look at others' success with jealousy. Instead, the sacrifice of thrift uses others' success as inspiration to stay focused on the vision!

Negotiation

When my daughter was thirteen, I asked her to read five books that I thought would help her become a better adult. Of course, there was pushback. I experienced the groaning and rolling of the eyes that teenage daughters are famous for. But she read a few of them anyway. One of those books was *The Five Lessons a Millionaire Taught Me About Life and Wealth* by Richard Paul Evans.

When she finished the book, I asked her, "What stuck out the most from the book? What was your biggest takeaway?"

She replied, "The seven golden words!"

I admit that was my favorite part of the book as well. The seven golden words are: *Is that the best you can do?* When negotiating with anyone about anything, I have found those words profoundly useful. They aren't high pressure or disrespectful. They are curious. Some of the most significant discounts I have received on vehicles, software, or houses have come from those seven golden words.

In my previous book, *The E-Hero's Guide to Real Estate Investing: Increase Your Cash Flow Without Increasing Your Workday*, I explained that negotiation depends on knowing what you want and being prepared. Negotiation is a must for the wealth behavior of thrift. It will help you maintain your budget by keeping your costs down (Moore 2022).

Negotiation isn't just about haggling with a salesperson. I see it as a factor whenever you are doing business with people.

In Spanish, the word for business is *negocio*, which literally means dealing with people. It is from the Latin *negotiationem*, business, or *negotiari,* to carry on business, to do business. In that sense, whether you are cutting coupons, buying off the clearance aisle, or haggling with a used car dealer, you're negotiating. For the sacrifice of thrift, every buying decision involves negotiation.

The sacrifice comes into play when sometimes you must either go without, or negotiate a deal on the purchase. I don't like going without, but there were many years that we did just that.

One year, to save money, Angela and I took our two oldest kids to San Antonio for a family vacation. Our plan was to go to Sea World and then Fiesta Texas. We stayed at a great hotel, a lot nicer than we were used to, all crammed into one room together.

That wasn't what was unusual about this vacation. I had calculated that for us to afford to go, we had to go in the off-season, October, and we could only afford to eat at McDonald's the whole trip.

It worked well, since our kids actually liked eating at McDonald's. I didn't have to hear them complain, didn't spend very much, and didn't have to tip! Thankfully for Mom and Dad (Angela and me), since we have been blessed financially, we don't have to go on those vacations anymore. I don't think my stomach could take the punishment now that I'm older.

As I said before, when negotiating with salespeople, you must know what you want. Specifically, you need to know what you want to accomplish, your price point, and your alternatives.

What you want to accomplish is less about the product you're buying and more about the need you're satisfying. The salesperson may have options available that you don't know about. You may want to tell the salesperson what you need and make them do the work to meet your need.

In Chris Voss's book with Tahl Raz, *Never Split the Difference: Negotiating as if Your Life Depended on It*, he suggested asking the opposing side questions like, "How can we get this done?" Those questions move the burden to the other side and sometimes spark creativity in the parties involved (Voss and Raz 2017).

You should figure out your price point before heading into negotiations. One of my friends, a used car dealer, told me, "When you go to an auction, it's easy to get caught up in the emotion and adrenaline of the bidding process—only to find if you win, you're the sucker who paid too much!" If you know your starting and ending price points before the negotiation, you're better prepared to stay disciplined and walk away when the price gets too high.

Sometimes, you need to find alternatives. Without alternatives, you're vulnerable during a negotiation. As Donald Trump says in his book, *Trump: The Art of The Deal*, "You must be prepared to walk away from the deal!" Having alternatives gives you this power in the negotiation (Trump and Schwartz 2016).

When I negotiate for real estate, generally, I look for two or three houses of a similar type to purchase. I may make simultaneous offers and see which seller is willing to negotiate. I will walk away at any time, even if I lose the earnest money. It is better to lose a small amount of cash than continue with a bad deal. Think about that money as the cost of making a good decision.

Budgeting

Early in our marriage, my wife and I struggled with money, as I shared. We battled constantly over who was to hold the checkbook and how financial decisions were made. Being the chauvinist male that I was, I believed it was my responsibility. However, whenever we needed supplies or groceries, Angela was the one who actually did the shopping. I would tell her an amount to spend, and she would laugh at me.

A vast disconnect existed between what I thought our budget should be and how much things actually cost. Angela is as thrifty as they come. No one could find bargains like her, with or without coupons. It didn't take long before I realized that the responsibility of the checkbook should be hers—and that I should consult with her about those areas of our monthly budget.

The checkbook responsibilities have changed over time, especially with the growth of our businesses. When we became entrepreneurs, I had to pay bills for the real estate and the firm, so it made sense for me to pay the bills for our personal account. She still purchases most of our groceries and supplies for the house, though. What hasn't changed is how we decide on our budget—together.

Like any couple, we have had disagreements, but the one place we must agree is around money. For us to function as a team, we had to create a budget based on our vision of where we wanted to be—financially free and with true wealth—and how we were going to get there.

If you're engaged to be married, be sure to have this discussion before getting a joint checking account and credit card. If you're single, writing down a budget and getting in the habit of reviewing it each month will get you on the right path.

Create your budget by first tracking your expenditures for the last three to six months. If you don't use an accounting or income-and-expense tracking software, you should. Many on the market allow you to download them onto your phone or tablet and can connect directly with your bank and credit card accounts.

Once you know where the money went in the past, decide where it will go in the future. Start with your monthly income, then from the list you prepared of your monthly income and expenses, subtract your expenses.

Start with the most essential expenses, like housing and transportation, then list the remaining categories. This is called *zero based budgeting.* It assumes any amounts not spent will be allocated to savings and investing. If you come to the end of your expenses and show a negative number, decisions must be made.

You may have to reduce your entertainment expenses, stop a few streaming subscriptions, or decide to eat at home more. Dining at restaurants and eating takeout usually represent your biggest opportunity for savings.

Speaking of savings, have you built that into your budget? We will talk more about savings and investing later, but for now, you should begin saving at least 10 percent of your income every month. Use your retirement plan or investment accounts, or build up your cash reserves or that first $1,000.00 of your emergency fund.

In his book, *Dave Ramsey's Complete Guide to Money,* Dave Ramsey recommends monthly budget meetings with your spouse (Ramsey 2011). Whether married or single, you should review the budget from the last month compared to your actual expenses and prepare the budget for the next month. When you budget this way, you tell your money what to do. You drive your financial train instead of being pushed around by the demands on your cash.

Savings

Saving isn't the same as investing. Saving has a specific purpose. Your savings should cover any emergencies and helps you avoid borrowing money for those emergencies. In other words, your savings exists to eliminate the need for credit cards.

Less than half of Americans have enough money saved to pay for an emergency of just $1,000. That's why you should begin your emergency fund by saving $1,000. If you haven't gone through *Financial Peace University* with Dave Ramsey, you should probably do so.

Our two oldest kids have gone through the class. My oldest son, Conner, went through the course with my wife and me when he was seventeen. He didn't want to be there, but he was grounded, and I made it part of the terms of the grounding.

Everyone in the class told him they were so glad to see him there. They went on and on about how they wished they had heard the lessons of the course when they were his age. It was great to see him just smile and thank them. His mom and dad had been financially independent for several years, but we still learned from the class and were happy to be there with Conner.

Saving can be difficult for the person trying to get out from under a mountain of debt. It's much better to start early and be consistent. When I started saving, I opened a savings account at a bank where I didn't have a checking account. I wired small amounts of money from my other accounts every week.

To withdraw money from that account, I had to drive to that bank and physically withdraw the money. They offered to combine it with a checking account with a debit card or checks, but that would have made it too easy to withdraw. I wanted to think about the withdrawal during the drive, while filling out the form, and then speaking to the teller.

Start saving by making small automatic deposits from your main account into a savings account. When the amounts are small, they're less noticeable. They create self-imposed scarcity in your account—subconsciously telling you that you have less to work with, so you need to conserve your cash.

How much should you save? Since saving has a purpose, you decide what limit to place on that account. I had a friend from church who saved 20–30 percent each pay period. When I met him, he had over $30,000 in cash reserves.

At some point, when your cash reserves are sufficient, you need to take the next step into investing. Except for his pension at work, my friend had no other investments. We will talk more about investing in the next chapter.

The right amount of reserves depends on how many months of expenses you feel comfortable keeping in cash. Most people will be satisfied with three months of expenses in reserve. Others will want to hold six months of expenses in cash. Before I was self-employed, I lost my job four times (see my previous books for those stories). So, I prefer to have at least six months of expenses in cash or liquid assets. Whatever your comfort level, the purpose of the cash reserve is to keep you from using consumer debt or credit cards. To enjoy financial freedom and true wealth, you can't be addicted to credit.

Getting Out of Debt

So how do you manage your current credit card debt? Getting out of debt requires using the wealth behavior of discipline and the debt snowball. The debt snowball method of debt reduction can rapidly eliminate your consumer debt from credit cards, vehicles, jet skis, or whatever you have accumulated before reading this book.

It's important to note that to get out of debt, you must stop adding new debt. That's why we discussed having an emergency fund first. Without the emergency fund of $1,000, when financial chaos comes, you rely on Visa or Mastercard instead of yourself.

First, create a list of all debts, starting with the smallest debt balances to the largest. Pay off the smaller balances first, regardless of their interest rates. The minimum payments should be made on all other balances. Allocate any additional free cash from your budget toward the smallest balance. Once it's paid off, then shift that free cash to the minimum payment of the next smallest balance.

As you continue paying off balances, the payments made on the smaller balances should be aggregated towards the next largest balance. You repeat the process until all balances are paid off. When you continue shifting the previous payments to the next largest balance, you create a "snowball" effect of paying off your debts faster than without a plan.

But don't stop there! Once all of your credit card and consumer debts are paid, including vehicles, take the payments that were going to your debt and *pay yourself!* Use that discipline to build up your cash reserves and eliminate your need to use a credit card again. Once you have enough cash to cover six months of expenses, you're now ready to begin investing.

The sacrifice of thrift wealth behavior makes your money your servant. Instead of floating on the waves of daily expenses, you become the master of your finances. As the first wealth behavior that focuses on money, this behavior will take time, faith, and patience to develop. Once you're in command, you're ready for the next wealth behavior: the power of investing!

Chapter Summary: The Sacrifice of Thrift

- Thrift tells your money what to do instead of allowing your bills to tell your money what to do.
- Thrift involves budgeting, saving, staying out of debt, and negotiating good deals.
- Comparison poisons the soul of the entitled, when we believe that we deserve something that someone else has.
- The good kind of comparison tracks your progress. It compares your current net worth, monthly cash flow from investments, relationships with your family, and leadership development, not to others but to where you were one, three, or five years ago.
- Negotiation depends on knowing what you want and being prepared. Every buying decision involves negotiation.
- Create your budget by tracking your expenditures for the last three to six months. Use an accounting or income and expense tracking software.
- Saving is not the same as investing, but it has a specific purpose: to cover any emergencies and help you avoid borrowing money for those emergencies.
- Getting out of debt requires using the wealth behavior of *discipline* and the debt snowball.
- Once all of your credit card and consumer debts are paid, including vehicles, take the payments that were going to your debt and *pay yourself!*

CHAPTER 8

THE POWER OF INVESTING

*"Be diligent to know the state of your
flocks and attend to your herds;
For riches are not forever, nor does a
crown endure to all generations."*
—Proverbs 27:23–24

In the fall of 2000, I became an investor. My wife and I bought our first residential rental property. I didn't know at the time how much my life would be impacted by that decision.

We were stressed out during the days before we found our first tenant and received the deposit and first month's rent. The money entered our account one day before the first mortgage payment due date.

I still remember their names. They were from Michigan. That proved lucky when the heater didn't work, and it took me a few days to get it repaired. They didn't mind the cold. As tenants, they were the best. They treated the house like they owned it. They even helped me figure out some plumbing issues.

For them, it was just a place to live. For me, it became my identity. I'm an investor. That house began a journey of faith that led to investing in one hundred other houses, mutual funds, exchange-traded funds, and CPA firms.

So far, I haven't addressed the verses from Proverbs at the beginning of each chapter. This one, however, is different. This verse, and the verses following it, speak of your "flocks" providing for you even when your "riches" disappear. I think "riches" here describes your income or savings—representing value received in the past.

Sheep and goat farming differs from other livestock in the products you harvest from them. Unlike raising crops, where once you harvest the produce, there is nothing more it can provide, sheep and goats can provide you with a lifetime of dividends. You reap their wool and mohair several times per year. Their milk will continue to flow if you take care of them. In addition, you can breed the livestock and sell lambs and kids (baby goats).

The writer of Proverbs wasn't just giving farm and ranching advice. In verses twenty-five through twenty-seven of the same chapter, the writer lays out all the benefits of this type of asset. Sheep and goats represent future earnings. Here the author describes what an investment looks like.

What Is an Investment?

An investment produces both income and appreciation over time. With an outlay of capital or money, the investor expects this asset to increase in value and provide income during its useful life. Investments can be made in real estate, oil and gas mineral interests, partnership interests, promissory notes, stocks, bonds (or their derivatives), small business interest, etc.

Earlier in the book, I said, "Saving is not investing!" Especially in low-interest-rate environments, savings accounts can't be considered investments. In high-interest-rate periods of the past, you could purchase a certificate of deposit (CD) and expect significant income. Those saving vehicles provide income over time, but they don't appreciate.

Today, CDs pay very little, and your money could lose buying power because of inflation. Let's say you put $100 in a CD that matures in twelve months, and the CD is offering a 1 percent annual interest payment of $1.00. If the inflation rate is 3 percent that year, you have lost 2 percent or $2.00 worth of buying power. Why? Because the stuff you wanted to buy at the beginning of the year priced at $100 now costs $103. This is an oversimplified example of inflation and buying power, but you get the point. Your investments should outpace inflation with either the income you receive or the increase in value of that investment.

Some things considered investments by many don't actually provide income as well as appreciate in value. They therefore fail my definition of an investment. Some examples of assets that might appreciate but pay zero income include artwork, rare coins, collectibles, and the like.

In addition, your personal residence does not qualify as an investment by my definition, even though many realtors will tell you otherwise. Yes, it should increase in value, but a house requires maintenance, property tax, insurance, and more expenses. Without income from the house to pay those expenses, you must pay them from your earnings.

Many people make money when they sell the property. However, unless you move out of your city or state, you will still need a place to live. If real estate prices have gone up 25 percent since you purchased your home, and you have a home worth $300,000, you will have to spend almost the same amount to purchase a similar quality home. At best, you could engage in a lateral move; at worst, with all the realtor fees and closing costs, you will lose money.

For your personal residence to be an investment, it would have to earn you more money than it costs you. There is a way to make that happen. It's called house-hacking. With house-hacking, you purchase a multi-family residence, maybe a duplex or quadruplex, and rent out the other units while living in one of them. In this case, the rental income you receive might be more than what the property costs you. And hopefully, it will appreciate in value over time.

Risk Management

Every investment involves some level of risk. The possibility of the investment not performing according to expectations or losing value rather than appreciating in value describes *risk*. Everyone manages risk differently. Generally, you invest in assets that reflect your aversion or acceptance of risk.

For example, I don't like driving on those overpasses in the Dallas-Fort Worth (DFW) area that reach over twenty stories into the air. My knuckles start to grip the steering wheel, my breath gets heavy, and I sweat underneath my eyeballs. In contrast, when I took lessons to become a private pilot, I loved the moment when I opened the throttle, reached fifty-five knots, and pulled back on the stick, raising the aircraft off the ground as it soared two-to-three thousand feet into the air.

Why my different responses? The airplane, a Cessna 172 single-engine propeller-driven craft, is designed to fly high off the ground. My car twenty stories up, if driven off the overpass, is designed to fall twenty stories. It makes perfect sense to me, but that illustrates my risk tolerance.

You also have a distinct level of risk tolerance or risk aversion. Find those investments that give you a good *return on investment* within your risk tolerance; maybe talk to your financial advisor. We will define return on investment later, but I would like to talk about how to find your risk tolerance for investing.

Looking at your vision and goals first, you will see the destination you want your investments to take you. That destination may be a net worth number or an income number, or both. Next, determine the time horizon you set for your investments to meet those goals. This creates a due date, retirement date, or some other self-imposed deadline for your investments and yourself to work with. Whatever age you begin investing, your time horizon and target retirement account balances will shape how aggressive you choose to be.

One of my real estate investor friends declared that his cash flow from residential rental properties would be sufficient for him to quit his job in two years. Because of his diligence and willingness to invest in real estate, he met that self-imposed deadline.

Now that you have your destination and deadlines, you should adjust your investment choices to the lowest amount of risk you can endure and still meet those targets. If the risk on those investments exceeds what you can emotionally and financially tolerate, you may need to adjust your time horizon or the destination.

When you invest in something you know nothing about, your emotions tend to be more involved. Very similar to the emotions seen while gambling in a casino, uninformed investing produces fear, anxiety, and pain. At the casino, people throw down stacks of chips that represent way more of their income than they should be risking and bet on something that has a very high probability of being lost. When they lose, and they will eventually lose, they're devastated. If your investing looks more like gambling, you're doing it wrong.

The way to battle those emotions involves the lifestyle of learning behavior in chapter 5. Whether you invest in the stock market, real estate, or something else, you need to educate yourself. I have so many people tell me that they don't know anything about the markets or their portfolios, yet they invest hundreds of thousands of dollars with me. Part of my job involves educating my clients on their investments and how market, economic, and political events can affect their investment growth. I encourage them to read and develop their understanding to become better investors.

Fear acts as the most significant barrier most people face when presented with an investment opportunity. Fear can keep you from receiving any return on investment, whether investing in a small business, passive income activity like real estate, or buying a portfolio of exchange-traded funds (ETFs). The sooner you begin investing, the more impact the time value of money can have on your portfolio!

Return on Investment

You calculate return on investment (ROI) by taking the annual income (i) plus the growth in value (g) divided by the investment made (n) (ROI = (i+g)/n). When calculating the growth in value, you must use a point-to-point method. Usually, the point-to-point includes a calendar year, rolling-twelve-months, investment-to-date. You can look those up on your own. For this book, we will stick to the calendar year method. This means that you compare the investment value on January 1, the beginning of the year, and December 31, the end of the year. For example, the growth in a stock valued at $100 on January 1 and then $110 on December 31 equals $10 or a 10 percent growth rate.

There are different ways to calculate ROI for different types of investments. Let's say you buy a stock for $100, like in the previous example, on January 1. During the year, it paid a $1 dividend each quarter, totaling $4. At the end of the year, the stock was worth $110. The ROI for that stock would be calculated as (4+10)/100 = .14 or 14 percent ROI.

For real estate, it gets a bit tricky. Since most people buy real estate with leverage or financing from a bank loan known as a mortgage, there are several ways to calculate ROI. Cash-on-cash return-on-investment (CocROI) uses your cash flow or net income from rental real estate, any change in market value of the property, and only the cash invested to calculate ROI.

What happens when you have a zero money-down property? Then your ROI calculation is infinite, incalculable.

To avoid this issue, some investors calculate their ROI using the cost of the property (including loans) plus closing costs, rehab costs, and the gross annual income rather than the cash invested and annual net cash flow. In addition, real estate investors will sometimes omit the change in value when calculating ROI until they sell the property.

Whatever method you use, the purpose is to compare one property to another to decide whether to make the investment. A simple ROI calculation helps identify great investments.

Lack of Resources

People often claim that they are limited by their lack of resources. They believe that a barrier exists between themselves and their dreams. They say lack of resources keeps them from moving forward. Yet you're only limited by your creativity.

When my father-in-law's grocery store was bought out again, we looked at his retirement account in disbelief. After thirty years of working in the grocery business, as I mentioned, he had little more than $6,000 in his 401k.

I didn't have any cash but had learned so much from my mentors about buying property and creating wealth through investing in real estate.

One day, we started talking, and he said he wanted to invest more in residential rental real estate to gain cash flow. Also, he hated working at the grocery store with the new management and needed a way out. I told him that I had learned quite a bit about real estate investing as a tax accountant and from my mentors, but that I needed capital to continue growing my investment portfolio. From that conversation, a partnership was born.

Partnerships help you overcome your lack of resources. You may have specific skills and abilities, while someone with capital is just waiting for you to call with a deal in mind. Form a partnership if you want to leverage a group of people's capital, resources, and skills. Not just for real estate, but many businesses start with two or more owners wanting to combine their strengths to overcome their weaknesses.

I once had clients who had started a restaurant. The three partners each brought something extraordinary to the business. One created a great atmosphere, developed the menu, and set the prices for each item. Another managed the business side including all the negotiations, dealing with vendors and contractors, and obtaining financing for the group. The third partner exuded creativity as the enterprise's head chef and public face. Since last I spoke to them, they had moved into several different markets and created eight unique and successful restaurants.

Partnerships create synergies where resources meet their full potential. Find people around you who share your values and want to invest. Join social media groups or local meetups to network with other investors. You overcome the lack of resources by connecting with others and seeing what you can accomplish together.

The Time Value of Money

What is the time value of money? An investment will grow exponentially because of the compounding effect of time—interest earned on interest or dividends that buys more shares that pay more dividends that buy more shares!

For example, let's consider two investors. The first investor we will name Bill, the second, Tom. Tom and Bill are both twenty years old. Bill decides he wants to start investing on his twentieth birthday at $1,200 per year at the beginning of each year. Tom decided to wait until his thirty-first birthday to begin investing the same amount annually until sixty-five years old. Both portfolios received the same return on investment each year of 8 percent. All interest and dividends were reinvested in both portfolios. On Bill's thirty-first birthday, he decided to stop investing altogether.

Who do you think had the most in their investment accounts at the end of their sixty-fifth year? Would it surprise you that even though Bill had only invested $13,200, his account had over $96,000 more than Tom's account? On their sixty-sixth birthday, Bill would have $318,957.60, whereas Tom would only have $223,322.58.

Now, what if Bill had continued investing until his sixty-fifth birthday? On his sixty-sixth birthday, he would have $542,280.18. Even though he only invested $13,200 more than Tom, he would have almost two and a half times more than Tom. And that is just the equivalent of $100 per month at an 8 percent ROI. Our example here was with annual contributions, but systematic monthly contributions over long periods of time will have similar results. Don't be like Tom. Start investing early, and start with whatever you can.

What if you are within fifteen years of retirement? Is it possible to make up lost ground? Absolutely! You may need to make more of a sacrifice to fund your investment and retirement accounts. Talk to a CPA, call our firm, or speak to your financial advisor.

Investing doesn't have to be complicated. You can start with $25 per month with some mutual funds. You just need to begin somewhere.

Alternative Investments

Sometimes investing in businesses might be the best place for you, especially if you know something about them. I have known people who invested in car washes and laundromats, because they are simple businesses once they are running—allowing you to deposit money while it operates largely on its own. It isn't that simple, but it's a passive business for the most part. You don't need many employees if any at all. When you invest in something like this, you should investigate the industry and find someone to help you analyze the costs.

I have purchased five accounting firms in the last twenty-something years. I have become an expert on buying accounting firms, not just for myself, but I know what to look for if others ask for my help. For you to become an expert at something, you need experience and education. Sometimes education comes from experience. That takes time and action.

Others have invested in limited partnerships (LP). Those LPs could be for oil and gas operations, or they might be for commercial real estate. You, the investor, need to do your due diligence before taking a stab at this type of investing. Most of the time, the operators of these LPs are looking for accredited investors. Accredited investors have a net worth of over one million dollars, not including their personal residence, and have an annual income of over $200,000 for the last two years ($300,000 for joint income).

These LPs may be regulated by the SEC and your state securities commission. The securities offered are often called *private placements* and are percentage ownership of the LP. An entity can also be considered an accredited investor if its assets exceed $5 million. Also, if an entity consists of owners who are accredited investors, the entity itself is regarded as an accredited investor.

Forced Savings and Forced Appreciation

If you invest in real estate on a long-term hold strategy, you may benefit from *forced savings*. As you pay down the loan on the property over time, you increase your equity in the property and your net worth. Real estate tends to appreciate over time, so the effect is exponential on your wealth. The use of debt to finance real estate when it produces passive income is called *leverage*. Read *The E-Hero's Guide to Real Estate Investing* for more information about investing in real estate.

Forced appreciation results when you buy a property under fair market value (FMV) that needs to be rehabbed to see its full potential. When you make small upgrades during the rehab, you can potentially increase the FMV much more than the costs you incur. For example, if the house was a two-bedroom, one bath with a bonus room, you might increase its value by turning that bonus room into a bedroom by adding a closet. This low-cost addition will yield a substantial increase in the FMV.

Seeing Opportunities

The wealth behavior of the power of investing requires you to look for and identify opportunities. How do you know what makes an investment opportunity? In my previous book, *The E-Hero's Guide to Real Estate Investing*, I said there's no such thing as a once-in-a-lifetime opportunity. They happen all the time. But how do you identify them?

First, you must be looking for them. If you think that the heavens will part, and a spotlight will show you the way, you're still sleeping and need to wake up from that nightmare. No, instead, look for possible sources of business sales. There are several business brokers around; join their newsletter or in their social media group. In addition, use your network to ask people if they know of any leads. This works for businesses and real estate.

Next, you want to have accountability partners to help you sift through the opportunities you find, determining if they are indeed opportunities. Accountability partners include business coaches, mentors, friend groups, CPAs, and attorneys. Those you trust will tell you the truth but won't steal your dreams with pessimism.

Be careful of the dream stealers. They hate to see anyone become successful, because it makes them look bad.

Retirement Versus Legacy

I know I said this wasn't a spiritual book, but I want to discuss a topic that is misunderstood by most Christians. It may surprise you, but the Bible never talks about saving and investing for retirement. That's an entirely twentieth-century American concept.

Retirement focuses on yourself—on your income, health, vacation, and lifestyle needs. Should you avoid retirement planning? No! Retirement planning also involves others, and as such should be part of an overall legacy plan. A legacy plan is focused on "leaving an inheritance to your children's children" (Proverbs 13:22). So you can see, the Bible does suggest the importance of financial planning!

Early in my career, I began to see how retirement planning fell short of what our clients needed. They were setting their sights too low to maintain their lifestyle and provide for their families after they hit age sixty-five.

By the way, I don't like using the term "retirement." The wealthy don't make plans to stop working. A few may want to retire, but that just means changing their vocation. The wealthy usually continue working on their investment portfolios, working with not-for-profits, or running their businesses until they can't physically do those things anymore.

In college, I worked for a "retired" business owner who had sold his business for several million dollars. His wealth clocked in at the eight-figure range. He invested in farming and ranching, storage units, securities, and for a brief time, rental real estate. He rented office space on the second floor of a bank in West Texas. Every day, he would go in to "work" to evaluate his investments, review his statements, and visit with me. Officially, my job was to reconcile all of his statements and track that his interest payments made it into his accounts. Unofficially, my job was to keep him company. He was over eighty years old and still very sharp. I learned so much from him. Retirement didn't mean anything to him.

Many financial planners will shoot for 80 percent of a client's current monthly income in retirement. Why? Well, your house should be paid off by then, and you need less money to live off. Again, who is this focused on? Self. If you plan to leave a legacy of wealth to your family, you should aim for a net worth number like $10 million. What happens if you only have $8 million when you can't work anymore? Well, I guess your family will have to figure out how make do with just $8 million. Setting your goals at the minimum needed to get by doesn't make sense. Set your aspirations to leave a legacy of wealth, instead of just trying to hit some retirement income number.

Legacy-minded people are outward-focused people. They are willing to work the *sacrifice of thrift* and use the *power of investing* not just for their financial independence but for the financial independence of generations to come. I want my grandchildren to know that they can pursue their dreams and have true wealth. They don't have to decide between their calling and paying the bills.

Legacy isn't about leaving the next generation things. Truly, things will pass away, rust, or decay. The legacy I am most concerned about revolves around these seven wealth behaviors. When my grandchildren ask their parents why they are so blessed, the answer should be because we learned how to build wealth from our parents. When you teach your kids the seven wealth behaviors, they can grow their inherited wealth exponentially—with each generation building on what the previous generations accomplished!

This leads us to our last wealth behavior, another reason we seek wealth and financial independence: to be a blessing.

Chapter Summary: The Power of Investing

- An investment produces both income and appreciation over time.

- Some things that are considered investments by many don't provide income as well as appreciate in value, so they fail to meet my definition of an investment.

- Every investment involves some level of risk. The possibility of the investment not performing according to expectations or losing value rather than appreciating in value describes *risk*.

- Risk tolerance depends on your vision and goals regarding how much time you have until you reach those goals, your time horizon. Some set their targets based on net worth or annual income, with their time horizon being at or near their "retirement age."

- Return on investment (ROI) takes the annual income (i) plus the growth in value (g) and divides it by the investment made (n) (ROI = (i+g)/n).

- Cash-on-cash return-on-investment (CocROI) uses your cash flow or net income from rental real estate, any change in market value of the property, and only the cash invested to calculate ROI.

- People often claim that they're limited by their lack of resources.

- Partnerships help you to overcome your lack of resources. You overcome the lack of resources by connecting with others and seeing what you can accomplish together.

- The time value of money is the idea that an investment will grow exponentially because of the compounding effect of time—interest earned on interest or dividends that buys more shares that pay more dividends that buy more shares!
- Sometimes investing in businesses might be the best place for you.
- *Forced savings* is when you pay down the loan on real estate over time. You then increase your equity in the property and your net worth. Real estate tends to appreciate over time, so the effect is exponential on your wealth.
- Forced appreciation results when you buy a property under fair market value (FMV) that needs to be rehabbed to see its full potential. Then you make minor upgrades during the rehab and potentially increase the FMV much more than the costs you incur.
- The wealth behavior of the power of investing requires you to look for and identify opportunities.
- Set your aspirations to leave a legacy of wealth instead of just trying to hit some retirement income number. Legacy-minded people are outward-focused.

CHAPTER 9

THE BLESSING OF GIVING

*"Do not withhold good from those to whom it is due,
when it is in the power of your hand to
do so. Do not say to your neighbor,
'Go, and come back, and tomorrow I will
give it,' when you have it with you."*
—Proverbs 3:27–28

In 2008, an associate pastor from a small town in West Texas took his family of seven around the country in their brand new, sixty-foot recreational vehicle (RV). They had sold their home and other investment properties to fund their next adventure—traveling the nation while observing and inquiring with as many churches and pastors as possible about their ministries. The pastor wanted to investigate why some churches connected with their communities and created leaders and disciples, while others didn't.

A year later, when they returned to that not-so-tiny West Texas town, they had no place to live. Since they were putting their RV up for sale, they had to keep it clean—which meant moving out of it.

Thankfully, one of their wealthy friends had a large home and offered to house them for a while. He and his wife had three kids of their own, so it was a sacrifice to share their space. After several months of looking for the right house for his family, the pastor hadn't found anything with enough bedrooms and bathrooms to house them all. The pastor's friend talked to his wife and prayed about it, then offered to sell them their home for what they owed on the property, giving the pastor all of their unrealized appreciation in the house. He even seller-financed it with little down and payments equal to his mortgage payments.

That may not sound like giving, but the friend's house was worth $60,000 to 80,000 more than what he sold it to the pastor for. Has anyone ever given you $60,000? Me neither. The friend knew that he was blessed to be a blessing (Genesis 12:1–3). His wealth and abundance had a purpose beyond himself.

Purpose for Wealth

Does wealth have a purpose? It should. If the only reason to acquire more income-producing assets consists of lining your pockets and filling your bank accounts, you will never be satisfied. When asked how much is enough, J.D. Rockefeller responded by saying, "Just a little bit more!" That kind of thinking leads to an empty life.

Remember, in chapter 2, I defined success as *enjoying what I do while having more than enough to meet my needs and the needs of others.* We will focus on the needs of others in this chapter.

Take a minute to look and see the needs around you. On second thought, take the next two weeks to ask yourself about the people you meet. What are their immediate needs? You may even ask them directly, telling them you're doing research. Then go home and write those needs down, categorize them, and ask yourself: *how can I help meet them?* Your next move is up to you.

Giving leads to a life full of purpose. Giving doesn't always refer to money, but also to time, values, and other resources. When you give, you will receive in kind. It is the law of sowing and reaping. When you sow a seed, you reap a plant or tree that produces hundreds, if not thousands, of other seeds. Let's go over the law of sowing and reaping in more detail.

Sowing And Reaping

The law of sowing and reaping dates back thousands of years. Some use the phrase, "what goes around comes around," while others use the term "karma." The idea is similar. If you do good to others, good returns to you—and the opposite is also true. We can divide the law of sowing and reaping into three distinct phases.

First, you always reap *what* you sow. When you plant sunflower seeds, sunflowers grow from those seeds. You can't reap almonds if you plant sunflowers. Therefore, be careful what seeds you plant. You must purpose to sow good into other people's lives. Don't act surprised when acquaintances don't want to hang around with you, after you have complained about them to others. Nor can you expect a positive response from your coworkers when you criticize them constantly. Instead, be mindful of your actions. Encourage people, compliment them, and find the good in everyone you meet. Those seeds will produce a harvest of many friends.

Second, you only reap *after* you sow. You can't harvest grain from mere good intentions. Until you actually do the work to till the fields and plant the seeds, nothing will grow but weeds.

Whenever a farmer plants a field, he trusts the ground to do its work in nourishing those seeds. He doesn't check on the seeds or dig them up to make sure the roots are sprouting. No, he sows, then he waters and waits. Sowing takes work.

Be intentional in your actions every day. Working towards your goals and choosing to be a blessing to those around you requires effort. The key here is to make that effort have positive lasting effects.

Selfish behavior and narcissistic tendencies take effort as well. Unfortunately, the result of that behavior destroys relationships and isolates the sower. You can gain the whole world, hoard all the world's wealth, and end up empty and lonely.

Finally, you always reap *more* than you sow. The farmer who toiled in the ground to plant the seed knows that each seed represents two types of harvest. One will be sold for money or traded for other goods and services, but the other will be kept back and used to plant next year. One sunflower can produce around one thousand seeds. That sunflower came from one of those seeds. In effect, each sunflower, from its seeds, represents a possible one million sunflower seeds. Reaping more than what you sow involves multiplication rather than just addition.

How does that translate to giving? Giving time, money, and resources tends to have a multiplying impact. When you give your time to train and develop one leader, and they train and develop two or three leaders, your time and effort have multiplied the number of leaders. When you give to an individual, they're often inspired to pay it forward. They may, in fact, pay it forward many times over from that one inspired gift.

Doing Good Versus Good Intentions

When I was still in college, I worked at an apartment complex as the night desk and auditor. During that job, I met several tenants when they would come in to pay their rents.

One family seemed to struggle every month with their rent and vehicle. Seeing them work on, and occasionally fail to start, their car made me want to do something for them. So, I decided to give them my car. This sounds like a good idea, right? Even though I still had two or three payments left on the note, and I had no idea how I would get another vehicle, against good counsel, I handed them the keys.

Of course, they were appreciative at first. Then the following week, they came to me complaining that the brakes went out. Since it was still in my name, I paid to fix the brakes. They never said, "Thank you." Then, as weeks went by, the car's condition quickly deteriorated. Finally, my car troubled them as much as their old car. Why? It didn't cost them anything, so they didn't value it enough to provide the necessary care and preventive maintenance. Also, some people don't take care of their belongings.

When you decide to be a do-gooder, focus on the results rather than your intentions. Doing good requires a good outcome. In my situation, several indicators showed that this "good deed" would not end well for both the donor and the recipient.

First, giving the car was much more of a sacrifice than prudent giving should allow. Even God only asks for 10 percent. Of my assets, I'd given more than 50 percent of my personal wealth (if you can call it that) when I gave away my car.

Also, I desperately needed a vehicle to get to school. Without a plan to meet that need, giving my car away left me in a bind.

Then, the recipients of my gift didn't show any indications that they would appreciate and value the gift. In fact, in their eyes, after the gift, I remained responsible for the car's maintenance. In the end, they were no better off than before I had given them my car. In essence, I didn't do good.

We will talk about how to *give well* later. Now let's look at some ways to see the results, instead of just making ourselves feel good with our intentions.

You should look for impact. If an organization or an individual will be the beneficiary of your gift, how will it impact their life? Giving money to panhandlers on the roadside likely will have no impact on their lives. Giving to an organization that trains people to learn various job skills changes lives.

Many organizations only deal with the symptoms of an issue. The wise giver looks deeper. You often hear stories of those who have received charity, later saying how thankful they are. But what happened after they received the gift or support? Did they need the same gift or support the following month as well? Any organization that gives ongoing support without requiring goals or improvements enables the problem to continue.

Also, how will this gift impact you? Those who give away their seed money have nothing to plant. In other words, if you give, give out of your abundance, not out of your need. When my wife, Angela, and I were young, we loved to give to others. Unfortunately, we, or maybe just I, didn't understand this principle. I would give my utilities money to someone I thought "needed" it, when I didn't really have it to give. Does it make sense to pay someone else's utilities and then need someone else to help you pay your own utilities? After giving the car and then giving to the church money that was supposed to go to the electric company, I remembered that giving should come from my abundance.

As I said in the introduction to the wealth behaviors, most of us live in the US live in abundance. If you have developed the behaviors of discipline and thrift, then you will know when you have enough to give to others. People who are acting selfishly spend everything they have on themselves, and then say they don't have enough to be a blessing to others.

Additionally, you should look at your motives for giving. Are you giving to satisfy a need, change someone's life, or keep animals from neglect? Or are you giving to get something in return—such as recognition from others—or to make yourself feel better? The latter centers around yourself. When people give like that, you can see their motives as much as you see their giving. Unselfish giving doesn't require an audience.

When you do good, the results are evident. You can measure the impact and see change.

Giving Well

Giving well requires thoughtfulness and planning. It rarely happens in haste. Hasty decisions usually end badly.

Often, charities or even churches rely on your emotional decision-making to outweigh your rational decision-making when it comes to giving. Have you ever been to a charity event where they discuss all the things the charity has done the previous year, and then they bring out someone who has been helped by the organization for one final plea? They know that emotion drives your wallet, not logic or reason. Even thoughtful, planned decisions happen because of your emotions. Before you write that check (for young people: a piece of paper representing a draw on your bank account), I ask that you sit down with your budget, your spouse, and anyone else to whom you might be accountable. As discussed in the previous section, you need to ask yourself several questions, which we will explore next.

What is my motivation? Your motivation may sincerely be to help the charity with its mission. Great. Still, you should ask the question of yourself. Not all motivations align with the charity's mission. Some people seek to gain favor with the leadership of the charity, community, or maybe even employer. You shouldn't feel bad or withhold the gift if that is your motivation. Building goodwill with others through giving can reap great rewards. Just be honest about it. Tell them the gift's purpose—that it's in their honor.

What is my budget? Like I stated before, giving comes from your abundance. You shouldn't donate your car payment or rent payment to a charity. When you neglect your responsibilities, you create chaos in your life. I recently listened to a podcast from a church going through a building program. They talked about a single mother who emptied her bank account and gave it to the church. The host said, "God told her to do it."

It's hard to argue with someone who says God told them to do something, unless you have some biblical reference that contradicts their statement. Would God say something like that?

There are two stories, in the Old and New Testaments, where God did just that. The context of those stories matters and is often overlooked. Both women had nothing left and no recurring revenue.

It would be hard to find anyone in the US that would fit that definition today. If you have a job, you should have a budget. That budget should be consulted before any charitable giving, period. Be wise. Sure, you can cut your daily, overpriced Starbucks latte for the next month and give to a charity instead. But when you take from your housing, transportation, and other vital categories, you become the person in need of charity.

Am I sowing in good ground? This is another Bible reference (see Mark chapter 4). In this story, Jesus describes four types of ground: the footpath, the shallow soil, the thorny ground, and the fertile soil. Without getting into the spiritual meanings of this passage (and there are many), let's focus on the differences between the first three compared to the fertile soil. The main difference lies in the results.

As I said, if the gift will not have a life-changing impact on the end-user, what is the point? Throwing money at something doesn't make it better. For example, our US government spending in 1980 per student (when adjusted for inflation to match 2018–2019 dollars) was $7,411. In 2015, we spent almost double that amount, $13,081 (NCES 2019). You would expect to see a significant increase in SAT average scores over the same period, right? You would be wrong. According to the College Board Report for 2015, the average SAT score in 1980 was 994 (Reading 502 + Math 492). However, the average SAT score in 2015 was 1006 (Reading 495 + Math 511), a difference of only twelve points in thirty years and almost double the spending. Clearly, spending more on "education" had little effect on how well our kids performed—leaving us to debate whether the increased spending had any positive impact.

How should I give? This question requires reflection. Giving allocates your resources to a charity, person, or group. Those resources may include your money, securities, objects, time, or knowledge. Like many entrepreneurs, you may see a need and want to do something about it. The choice becomes, what will you do about it? Let's go over each of those types of gifts individually.

Money. According to the Giving USA Annual Report, Americans gave a record $471 billion to charity in 2020, a 5 percent increase over 2019. Interestingly, that happened during the COVID-19 pandemic, when most Americans were stuck at home (GivingUSA 2021). It seems that we aren't as self-centered as the media and the rest of the world like to make us out to be.

As a method of giving, cash giving involves the least amount of difficulty. With auto drafting from bank accounts and the use of the internet, charities remove most barriers to this method. My regular donations automatically get drafted from my account or charged to a credit card (that I pay off every month). If you don't pay off your credit card every month, please use your debit card instead. Don't give to charity only to pay interest on the accumulated debt.

Securities and Real Property. Many investors choose to give securities and real property directly to charity for the tax benefits. With appreciated investments like these, an individual receives a tax deduction for the asset's fair market value (FMV). In effect, the investor avoids capital gain taxes on the investment's value over what the investor paid for the asset. The charity can sell the assets, securities, or real property, and as a non-profit entity, they're exempt from any tax on the sale. It's a good strategy for regular givers who own appreciated assets.

Objects. This category includes vehicles, furniture, computers, machinery, clothing, jewelry, and countless other "things." Like securities and real property, the giver receives a tax deduction on the FMV of the asset, rather than the cost. Since the value isn't available on an open market, an appraisal is required by the Internal Revenue Service (IRS) for anything over $5,000. Talk to your tax advisor about the tax benefits of giving. When giving "things" to a charity, don't give junk! Don't give a church broken computers or the Salvation Army clothes with holes and stains. Slightly used clothing makes a great gift to the Salvation Army or Goodwill, but throw it in the garbage if it has holes or stains.

Time. Your time is your most valuable resource. When you give that resource to a charitable organization, you align yourself with that organization. You say to those whom you serve that you care by volunteering.

In churches, financial giving usually follows volunteering. When people volunteer, they connect with a new community of like-minded people. It becomes a heart connection with that cause or organization.

Unfortunately, some organizations take advantage of their people by working them like employees instead of stewarding their volunteers. Being a steward means that you know the boundary between hired help and a loving giver. You, as a volunteer, need to communicate with the organization about those boundaries as well. If you do, volunteering produces a tremendous amount of joy.

Many people who have a desire to help and "change the world" don't know where to start. I once heard a leader on a podcast say that they couldn't reach all women, but they could reach one woman. Start with one. You may have a desire to see at-risk youth develop as leaders. Don't quit your job; go to the Girls & Boys Clubs in your city, and mentor one kid. If what you want to do doesn't exist, start something. Start small and see what happens. You would be surprised at the impact you can make in peoples' lives by just spending time with them.

Knowledge. Do you think about releasing the knowledge and experience to others as giving? Probably not, but it is. There are many ways that people choose to do this. On YouTube, an experienced dad teaches young people how to do things like tying a tie, replacing a tire, changing the oil on their car, and many other things. This is giving! Many young people today grow up without fathers. This dad, Rob Kenney, can be found by searching *Dad How Do I?* or clicking the link https:// www.youtube.com/c/DadhowdoI. To read the comments, you can see how much of an impact he has made by sharing his knowledge.

I write books to give my kids and others the value of my experiences, victories, and mistakes. Passing on what you know doesn't have to be through social media or a book. It can involve just sharing with others. The world we live in today gives us so many opportunities to share knowledge. The possibilities are endless with blogs, YouTube, other video platforms, self-publishing, and social media.

Again, be careful to check your motivation. Sharing knowledge to promote yourself puts people off. Sharing because you want to solve a problem brings people in. Knowledge sharing implies that you have experience and information others need to know.

I wanted to write a book on real estate investing for years, but didn't. Why? I had read several books on real estate and didn't think I had anything new to add. Then a friend made a casual statement at lunch one day. He said, "Brandon, you might have similar information, but no one else will have your perspective, your voice."

Wendy K. Walters, author of *Marketing Your Mind, Brand Yourself, Write Your Book, Build Your Platform*, said, "Everyone has something to say about something!" Give your knowledge to the world, or your friends and family, by writing it down.

Leaving a Legacy

We already discussed the different motivations for investing: retirement versus legacy. Here, I want to expand on that idea. What is your legacy? What is your family identity? As we end this chapter on the blessing of giving, I admonish you to sit down and write your eulogy. What do you want people to say about you when you are gone?

Make a list, write out bullet points, and use a mind map. It doesn't matter how you get there. Once you have the list, do everything in your power to make it happen. Since you can't take your wealth with you, find its purpose. Your legacy is the sum of all your life's activities, good and bad. Make it a good one.

Chapter Summary: The Blessing of Giving

- Giving leads to a life full of purpose and meaning. Giving isn't just in money, but in time, values, and other resources.

- Sowing and reaping date back thousands of years. Some use the phrase, "what goes around comes around," while others use the term "karma." The idea is the same. If you do good to others, good returns to you.

- You reap what you sow, after you sow, and more than you sow. Giving time, money, and resources tends to have a multiplying impact.

- When you decide to be a do-gooder, focus on the results rather than your intentions. Doing good requires a good outcome.

- When you do good, the results are evident. You can measure the impact and see change. Good intentions usually make things worse and create unintended consequences.

- Giving well requires thoughtfulness and planning. It rarely happens in haste. Hasty decisions usually end badly.

- Giving allocates your resources to a charity, person, or group. Those resources may include your money, securities, objects, time, or knowledge.

- Your legacy is the sum of all your life's activities, good and bad.

CHAPTER 10

THE CONCLUSION

"The soul of a lazy man desires and has nothing;
But the soul of the diligent shall be made rich."
—Proverbs 13:4

In the introduction, I talked about growing up in Irving, Texas, and thinking that my only chance at wealth depended on my skill at baseball or going to Hollywood to be a star. Thirteen-year-old me would not even have imagined my life today. If there was a case for the opposite of these wealth behaviors, it was me. Thankfully, my life changed at age nineteen, when I gave my heart and life to Jesus.

The path towards success and eventually wealth took some time. Many bad habits and behaviors needed removing. Before, I practiced the art of self-destruction. After, I learned to practice continuous self-improvement. I read very little before, but was encouraged to read the Bible and other books after. I thought my career path included ministry somehow. It wasn't until after I graduated college that I discovered that I could help more people by becoming a certified public accountant (CPA).

During college and my first few years as an accountant, I began to see the wealth behaviors lived out in front of me. Various mentors, clients, or friends had stories of their own—going from nothing to millionaire status. I noticed the patterns of behavior shared by all of them and wanted what they had: financial independence. As I wrote in chapter 2, *true wealth is having enough income-producing assets and avoiding liabilities to enjoy financial independence and freedom from the stress of day-to-day money issues.*

From graduating college at age twenty-six to my net worth crossing the $1 million mark at age thirty-five, then the $5 million mark at forty-two, I have seen firsthand how these behaviors pave the way towards true wealth. It wasn't immediate, but it did happen through diligent adherence to the *seven wealth behaviors.*

Summary of the Wealth Behaviors

We started this journey by defining the differences between wealth and new-money-rich high-income earners. If you spend every dollar that comes in, you won't be wealthy. In fact, many high-income earners spend *more* than what comes in. Since they have high incomes, credit card companies happily give them high-limit accounts. This deficit spending continues until they refinance their house or declare bankruptcy.

Your net worth equals your assets minus your liabilities. Those new-money-rich folks you see on TV may have negative net worth, unless they employ a financial advisor who will tell them the truth.

To get from where you are now to where you want to be, you must have the *focus of vision*. This vision takes your dreams and helps translate them into reality. Your vision, through your skills and capabilities, fashions a plan that only you can accomplish. You should write down your dream, create goals, set due dates, and put action to those goals. The vision is just the beginning.

After vision, you learned about the *bridge of discipline* as a wealth behavior. Discipline connects what you desire to your joy like a bridge. Discipline includes consistency, constancy, and patience. These build your reputation as someone others can trust. Discipline also involves managing your time—scrubbing out waste from your schedule and blocking time for your priorities.

The *seven wealth behaviors* require you to have a *lifestyle of learning*. To walk out this educational journey, you need humility. From books, podcasts, blogs, mentors, and coaches, you learn how to create, manage, and expand your wealth. But learning must lead to experience. You must activate what you learn.

From learning to activation, you need to make good decisions. Knowing what to do and how to act on what you learn is *the value of wisdom*. Wisdom means making good choices, comprehending the seasons of life, and understanding people. You can have a great plan, yet fail miserably if it's not the right time. You could hit hardships and quit the journey before your breakthrough comes. You could start towards the mountaintop, only to see those around you abandon you. The value of wisdom helps to avoid those failures.

Next, you learned the first of three behaviors directly tied to your money. The *sacrifice of thrift* prepares for your desired future. Thrift rejects comparing yourself to others and focuses on what you can do right now. You squeeze all the power out of your dollars through negotiation, budgeting, and saving—while storing up a reserve for the unexpected. You command your money to obey you.

Once you build your reserves, it's time to release the *power of investing*. Understanding what investments look like will help you choose the type of investment that's right for you. In all investments, there are risks. Manage your risk based on your tolerance level. You learned how to calculate return on investment (ROI), and that lack of resources can't keep you from investing. As you understand the time value of money, you also understand that it hurts to wait.

Finally, you learned about the *blessing of giving*. That wealth has a purpose. You learned about the principle of sowing and reaping, and the difference between doing good versus having good intentions. You learned how to give well, and that a legacy of generosity can be your family's identity.

What Is Your Next Step?

So now what? In a world where you are bombarded with commercials that tell you how you can be happy, be the person who turns off the TV.

Years ago, I worked as the youth pastor and administrator for a small church in Lockhart, Texas. On one of my days off, I received a call from a lady at our church. As a single parent with two or three children, she called to ask for advice.

"Do you think I should trade in my car and buy another one?" she asked.

Puzzled by the question, especially to a youth pastor like me, I asked her, "Why do you want to buy a car?"

She said she had just paid off the previous car, and that since it was Labor Day, the dealerships were running sales.

I asked if she had any problems with her current vehicle. Did she spend a lot of money per month on repairs?

She said no.

Suddenly, I understood what to say. I told her, "I'm not going to tell you whether to trade in your car for another one. That's not my place. I will say, turn off your TV and radio for a week. During that week, pray and ask God for his wisdom. Read a chapter of Proverbs every day during this week, and then tell me what you think God is saying."

At the time, almost every commercial in that area on TV and radio were for car dealerships. I knew that those voices in her head were clouding out wisdom. They were pushing her to make emotional decisions. Whether she did what I suggested was irrelevant; what I wanted her to do was spend more time thinking about her decision. It may well have been the right decision to trade her car in. Without changing her behavior, however, she wouldn't have been able to make that decision well.

Changing your behavior will change your life. These seven wealth behaviors, when acted upon, lead to financial independence and true wealth. Like I said before, they are not new. As evidenced by the verses in Proverbs, this knowledge has been around for a long time.

Connect with the Author

As a CPA, financial advisor, and real estate investor for over twenty years, I have seen these *seven wealth behaviors* work in my life and the lives of my clients and friends. Like athletes training for a major competition, the wealthy practice these behaviors as they grow their net worth.

Behaviors consist of repeated thoughts and repeated actions. I don't like the saying *fake it until you make it!*, but the behavior comes first.

We discussed in the introduction that 70 percent of lottery winners end up in bankruptcy. According to *Sports Illustrated* article, *How and Why Athletes Go Broke*, 2009, 78 percent of former NFL players have gone bankrupt or are under financial stress after retiring for two years; 60 percent of NBA players are broke within five years of retirement (Torre 2009). It's not enough to have high income.

Even if you have a modest income, these wealth behaviors will work for you. You don't have to continue your life of living paycheck-to-paycheck. If you begin walking out the *seven wealth behaviors*, you will experience true wealth. I want that for you, your children, and your children's children.

If you need to make a change, connect with me at www.brandonkmoore.com. These behavior changes you make today will have a lasting impact. Let our firm help you with your financial plan, financial coaching, real estate coaching, and business coaching. If you would like me to speak at your event, please reach out to me. We want to see more people live a life of true wealth.

WORKS CITED

"2021 Poverty Guidelines." Office of the Assistant Secretary for Planning and Education. U.S. Department of Health and Human Services, 2021. https://aspe.hhs.gov/topics/poverty-economic-mobility/poverty-guidelines/prior-hhs-poverty-guidelines-federal-register-references/2021-poverty-guidelines.

Chapman, Gary D. *The 5 Love Languages: The Secret to Love That Lasts.* Vereeniging, SA: Christian Art Publishers, 2017.

Chapman, Gary D., and Paul E. White. *The 5 Languages of Appreciation in the Workplace: Empowering Organizations by Encouraging People.* Chicago, IL: Northfield Publishing, 2012.

Clear, James. *Atomic Habits: Tiny Changes, Remarkable Results:* London, UK: Random House Business Books, 2018.

"Digest of Education Statistics, 2019." National Center for Education Statistics. U.S. Department of Education, 2019. https://nces.ed.gov/programs/digest/d19/tables/dt19_236.55.asp.

El Issa, Erin. "Nerdwallet's 2021 American Household Credit Card Debt Study." NerdWallet, January 11, 2022. https://www.nerdwallet.com/blog/average-credit-card-debt-household.

"Empathy." Wikipedia. Wikimedia Foundation, June 6, 2022. https://en.wikipedia.org/wiki/Empathy.

Evans, Richard Paul. *The Five Lessons a Millionaire Taught Me about Life and Wealth.* New York, NY: Simon & Schuster, 2006.

Ferriera, Fransisco, and Carolina Sanchez-Paramo. "A Richer Array of International Poverty Lines." World Bank Blogs. World Bank, October 13, 2017. https://blogs.worldbank.org/developmenttalk/richer-array-international-poverty-lines.

Hanson, Melanie. "Student Loan Debt Statistics [2022]: Average + Total Debt." Education Data Initiative, May 30, 2022. https://educationdata.org/student-loan-debt-statistics.

"In 2020, Americans Gave $471.44 Billion to Charity, a 5.1% Increase over 2019." GivingUSA. The Giving Institute, 2021. https://givingusa.org/wp-content/uploads/2021/06/GUSA2021_Infographic_Digital.pdf.

Kenney, Rob. "Dad, How Do I?" Dad, How do I?'s YouTube Channel. YouTube, April 2020. https://www.youtube.com/c/DadhowdoI.

King James. Houndmills, Basingstoke, Hampshire, UK: Palgrave Macmillan, 2003.

Maher, Michael J. *The Seven Levels of Communication: Go from Relationships to Referrals*. Dallas, TX: BenBella Books, Inc., 2016.

Max, Tucker. "The Simple 5-Step Book Writing Plan." Scribe Media, June 9, 2021. https://scribemedia.com/5-step-book-writing-plan/.

Moore, Brandon K. *The E-Hero's Guide to Real Estate Investing: Increasing Your Cash Flow Without Increasing Your Work Day*. BKM Publishing, 2022.

Moore, Brandon K. *The E-Hero's Journey: Your Guide to the Entrepreneur's Quest*. BKM Publishing, n.d.

Murray, Theresa Dixon. "Why Do 70 Percent of Lottery Winners End up Bankrupt?" *Cleveland Plain Dealer*, January 14, 2016.

Ramsey, Dave, host. "What it Means to Live Like No One Else." The Ramsey Show (podcast). February 19, 2018. https://www.youtube.com/watch?v=Tom_PeRvgiI

Ramsey, Dave. *Baby Steps Millionaires: How Ordinary People Built Extraordinary Wealth-and How You Can Too*. Franklin, TN: Ramsey Press, The Lampo Group, LLC, 2022.

Ramsey, Dave. *Dave Ramsey's Complete Guide to Money*. Brentwood, TN: Lampo Liscensing, LLC, 2011.

Ramsey, Dave. *Dave Ramsey's Financial Peace University: Bankruptcy Edition*. Brentwood, TN: Lampo Group, Inc., 2005.

Roser, Max, and Esteban Ortiz-Ospina. "Global Extreme Poverty." Our World in Data. University of Oxford, May 25, 2013. https://ourworldindata.org/extreme-poverty.

Schoch, Marta, and Christoph Lanker. "The Number of Poor People Continues to Rise in Sub-Saharan Africa, despite a Slow Decline in the Poverty Rate." World Bank Blogs. World Bank, December 16, 2020. https://blogs.worldbank.org/opendata/

number-poor-people-continues-rise-sub-saharan-africa-de-
spite-slow-decline-poverty-rate.

"The Seven Wastes of Lean Manufacturing." EKU Online. Eastern
Kentucky University, July 22, 2020. https://safetymanagement.
edu/blog/the-seven-wastes-of-lean-manufacturing/.

Shakespeare, William. *As You Like It*. London, UK: Edward Blount,
William Jaggard and Isaac Jaggard, 1623.

Stanley, Thomas J. *The Millionaire Mind*. London, UK: Bantam, 2002.

Stanley, Thomas J., and William D. Danko. *The Millionaire Next Door:
The Surprising Secrets of America's Wealthy*. Lanham, MD: Taylor
Trade Publishing, 2016.

Star Wars Episode IV: A New Hope. Film. United States: Lucasfilm Ltd, 1977.

"Supercharge Your Strategic Planning; a High Performance
Process for Accounting Firms." Mindshop, June
23, 2021. https://web.mindshop.com/2021/06/21/
high-performance-planning-process-for-accounting-firms/.

Szymczak, Michal, Martyna Brozynska, Anna Lis, and Krzysztof Kowal.
5-Whys: Method First Handbook. 2K Consulting, 2016.

Torre, Pablo S. "How and Why Athletes Go Broke." *Sports Illustrated* 110,
no. 12, March 23, 2009.

Trump, Donald, and Tony Schwartz. *Trump: The Art of the Deal*. London,
UK: Random House Business, 2016.

Voss, Chris, and Tahl Raz. *Never Split the Difference: Negotiating as If Your
Life Depended on It*. London, UK: Cornerstone, 2017.

ABOUT THE AUTHOR

Brandon Moore is a CPA, Certified Wealth Strategist©, coach, and real estate investor who equips others to thrive in reaching their financial goals. Like many successful entrepreneurs, however, Brandon's career path hasn't been direct. The curves in his route have defined his success—while deepening his expertise.

Brandon didn't graduate at the top of his high school class. Instead, he lost his only run at student council, and a bout of pneumonia gave him an early (and perhaps fortuitous) opportunity to drop out of college (without grief from his father, he says).

After working as a janitor, losing a job as a life insurance agent, and serving as church youth director and eventually bookkeeper, Brandon decided to pursue a new career: that of an accountant.

Brandon then graduated from Angelo State University and began investing in real estate—buying and managing over

100 houses. A few years after graduating college, he acquired his CPA designation, and at age thirty-one, bought his first CPA firm—while building his real estate empire. Later, he purchased another four accounting practices. And during the 2008 recession, he acquired his financial service licenses to better serve CPA clients. He passed the Series 7, Series 66, and Life Insurance Agents license tests and has consistently remained in the top five to ten advisors of his broker/dealer.

Today, Brandon advises clients on wealth management—including charitable giving, estate planning, tax planning, retirement planning, investment allocation, risk management, and more. Brandon and his wife of twenty-five years, Angela, invest in and manage single-family properties and duplexes in West Texas. They have four children, who have been involved in the real estate business from early on.

Beyond the certifications and accolades, Brandon believes his purpose is to coach and develop leaders. He wants his family, friends, and clients to become their best selves, which is why he writes books and runs his podcast, "Coaching for Profit." He says, "I may only be able to coach a handful of people per day, week, or month. But these books can reach people exponentially."

In his free time, Brandon loves music and plays multiple instruments—often in his church. Brandon also recently reached his goal of third-degree black belt in Taekwondo, believing that martial arts offer a continuous improvement philosophy—training both mind and body.

Connect with Brandon at www.brandonkmoore.com.

THE E-HERO'S
JOURNEY

Your Guide to the Entrepreneur's Quest

AVAILABLE NOW ON AMAZON.COM

THE E-HERO'S GUIDE TO
REAL ESTATE INVESTING

Increase Your Cash Flow
Without Increasing Your Work Day

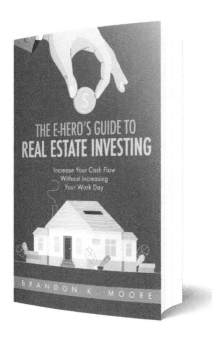

AVAILABLE NOW ON AMAZON.COM